COLOURS OF SOME CANADIAN BATTALIONS ON WOLFE'S MONUMENT IN
WESTMINSTER ABBEY

The 116th Batt. Colours are in the centre. These colours were worked
and presented to the Battalion by the ladies
of Ontario County

THE 116TH BATTALION IN FRANCE

BY
THE ADJUTANT

1921

The Naval & Military Press Ltd

Published by
The Naval & Military Press Ltd
5 Riverside, Brambleside, Bellbrook
Industrial Estate, Uckfield, East Sussex,
TN22 1QQ England

Tel: +44 (0) 1825 749494
Fax: +44 (0) 1825 765701

www.naval-military-press.com
www.nmarchive.com

In reprinting in facsimile from the original, any imperfections are inevitably reproduced and the quality may fall short of modern type and cartographic standards.

PREFACE

WITH the assistance of the official "War Diary" and the proud memory of two years' service with the 116th Battalion C.E.F. in France, the writer has compiled this small book for all ex-members of the Battalion, with the hope that they may find somewhere within its pages the reminiscence of days spent together, battles fought, and friendships made; and for the parents, relatives, and friends whose loved ones fell whilst fighting in the ranks of the Battalion, as a token of remembrance and sympathy.

THE ADJUTANT.

CONTENTS

	PAGE
INTRODUCTION	7
CHAPTER I.—SOMEWHERE IN FRANCE	13
CHAPTER II.—VIMY RIDGE	19
CHAPTER III.—UMPTY UMPS	27
CHAPTER IV.—THE RAID	31
CHAPTER V.—HILL SEVENTY	40
CHAPTER VI.—PASSCHENDAELE	49
CHAPTER VII.—REST BILLETS	53
CHAPTER VIII.—AUGUST 8TH	62
CHAPTER IX.—THE BOIRY SHOW	72
CHAPTER X.—CAMBRAI	82
CHAPTER XI.—MONS	88
HONOR ROLL	94

INTRODUCTION

THERE were very few, if any, Canadian Militia Regiments that succeeded in keeping their identity in France throughout the Great War. The reasons for this were—Firstly, the recruiting system, by means of which men were gathered into the Battalions of the Expeditionary Force, through the different Militia Regiments; the majority of the overseas Battalions being formed by drafts from three, four, five and sometimes more different Regiments. Secondly, the method of reinforcement, which distributed officers and men to Battalions in France disregarding any other principle except that these officers and men were from the same Province as the Battalion to which they were going. And even this did not hold good at all times.

The fact remains, however, that the 116th Battalion was recruited and fostered in the County of Ontario and led to France and in France by an officer of the 34th Regiment. In consequence, a few details concerning the military history of that County and the parent regiment may be of interest to those members of the 116th who joined the Battalion from other parts of the Province and through other regiments.

INTRODUCTION

The County of Ontario can justly claim credit to have been one of the first counties in the Province to recognize and fulfil its militia obligations, the first company of militia in the County being formed at Oshawa and known as The Oshawa Rifle Company.

Lieut. Colonel Bick, the Commanding Officer of the 34th Regiment, has in his possession a bugle with the following inscription:

"Presented by the Ladies of Oshawa to the Oshawa Rifle Company on their return home from the Front, June 1866."

The 34th Ontario County Regiment was organized in accordance with the general orders of September 14th, 1866, and was composed of ten companies and H.Q. as follows:—

Battalion and Staff H.Q............Whitby
No. 1 Company......................Whitby
    2   "   ....Brooklin
    3   "   ....Oshawa
    4   "   ....Greenwood
    5   "   ....Port Perry
    6   "   ....Uxbridge
    7   "   ....Beaverton
    8   "   ....Pickering
    9   "   ....Columbus
    10   "   ....Cannington

Sometime afterwards the Battalion was reduced to seven companies, those at Greenwood, Port Perry and Columbus being eliminated.

INTRODUCTION

In 1905 one more Company was added with Headquarters at Brechin and the distribution at the present time is as follows:—

Regimental H.Q. .... Whitby
A. Company .... Oshawa
B.   "   .... Whitby
C.   "   .... Oshawa
D.   "   .... Beaverton
E.   "   .... Uxbridge
F.   "   .... Port Perry
G.   "   .... Cannington
H.   "   .... Oshawa.

During the Fenian Raids of 1866 and 1868, Ontario County contributed its quota and a number of Ontario County men saw service in the North-West Rebellion of 1885, some of whom are still living in the County.

When war broke out in August, 1914, recruiting centres were established throughout Ontario County, and almost immediately the 34th Regiment was asked to supply a draft of 125 men for the First Contingent.

So great was the response to the call for this draft that finally 7 officers and 200 other ranks went to Valcartier to join the 2nd and 4th Battalions.

During the interval between the departure of the First Contingent and the enrolling of the Second, a great deal of preparatory work was done, but recruiting was not the only military activity of the times, as there was considerable anxiety felt throughout the County regarding the attitude of the alien population.

INTRODUCTION

The public buildings throughout the County were placed under guard, and upwards of 300 aliens were paroled and kept under surveillance. Great credit is due to Major A. F. Hind, at that time Chief of Police in Oshawa and later an officer in the 116th Battalion, for the efficient way in which this work was carried on.

During the month of May, 1915, Lieut. Colonel Bick, Officer Commanding the 34th Regiment, prior to his departure for Niagara with the 37th Overseas Battalion, appointed Captain G. W. P. Every of Whitby (later transferred to the 116th Battalion), to carry on recruiting throughout the County. Many small drafts of officers and men were despatched to the different overseas Battalions at that time being formed, including 27 other ranks to the 58th Battalion which was afterwards closely connected with the 116th in France; and so things went along until October, 1915, when the 116th Ontario County Battalion was authorized. Major S. S. Sharpe, second in command of the 34th Regiment, was given the command of the Battalion. Headquarters were established at Uxbridge with companies distributed as follows:—

A. Company......Uxbridge........Major H. P. Cooke
B. " ......Beaverton......Major F. H. Moody
C. " ......Whitby.........Major G. W. P. Every
D. " ......Oshawa.........Major A. F. Hind

Lieut.-Colonel Sharpe immediately set to work to enlist the sympathy and secure the co-operation of the citizens in all parts of the County.

A Civilian Recruiting League was formed and a

INTRODUCTION 11

deputation sent to wait upon the County Council and ask for financial assistance. The County Council responded in a magnificent manner to the request and voted $5,000 to the 116th Battalion—$2,000 for the purchase of band instruments, and $3,000 for recruiting purposes.

Many other generous donations were made to the Battalion by the people of Ontario County including the Colours of the Battalion, which were carried through Belgium, with great pride, after the Armistice.

The progress made in recruiting during the winter was such that by May, 1916, the Battalion was 1,145 strong, and on the 23rd of July, 1916, set sail from Halifax for England on the old reliable H.M.T. "Olympic."

Lt.-Col. S. S. Sharpe, D.S.O.

CHAPTER I.

SOMEWHERE IN FRANCE.

ON the 8th February, 1917, the 116th Battalion, quartered at Witley Camp, England, was warned to proceed to France on Sunday, 11th February. Everything, in consequence, was hustle and bustle, and the Battalion Orderly Room, which at the best of times is no haven of rest, was inundated with requests for additional information and leave. There was very little information to be got, other than that we were really for duty in France, and absolutely no leave, and so we gradually subsided and commenced preparations for our departure.

The next few days seemed an eternity, for it was greatly feared that, even though we had received official warning for France, the Battalion's departure might be delayed on account of mumps; at least four huts just now being quarantined with that disease. Notwithstanding many pessimistic prophecies emanating from the M.O. (Capt. James Moore), the fateful day arrived, and the Battalion, less its horses and half the transport section, which had been sent on in advance under Lt. Proctor, entrained at Milford Station at the usual army hour for such operations (1.10 a.m.), one ten ack emma.

The London and South Western Railway seemed determined to make up for all its past bad behaviour, and by ten o'clock the same morning we were all safely tucked away on board His Majesty's Transport "Victoria" with part of the 66th Imperial Divisional Headquarters and some drafts. Nothing of any importance happened during the voyage, and no "subs" were sighted, so far as we knew, so that by noon we had arrived at Boulogne. A short march brought us to St. Martin's Camp, during which we were carefully scrutinized by the inhabitants, who shouted many unintelligible comments at us, but which by the expressions on their faces we interpreted to be of a complimentary nature. A host of small, stockingless boys accompanied us all the way from the boat to the camp, asking the most extraordinary questions in broken English, and generally ending by "cigarette?" or "bully beef?".

St. Martin's Camp, situated as it was on the side of a hill, and about five kilometres from Boulogne, did not commend itself to us in any way, and there was nothing of interest there except the odd Y.M.C.A. or Salvation Army Hut. The men slept about ten in a tent and the officers were billeted all together in a kind of barn; blankets and bed rolls were freely distributed, and having vainly applied for leave to visit the City we turned in to dream of our dear ones or to wonder what fate had in store for us during the next few months. There is nothing on earth quite so trying as waiting for

SOMEWHERE IN FRANCE

orders, especially when confined to a camp like St. Martin's, but we were not to be kept in suspense very long, for at midnight (which, as has been mentioned before, is about the usual Army hour for such things) orders were received to move, and by 8 a.m., 12th February, the whole Battalion had entrained for a destination "Somewhere in France."

The poor old despised London and South Western Railway was a perfect paradise to the cattle trucks of this train, but what did anything matter now?

By 8 a.m. the following morning we had detrained at Houdain, at that time the centre of the rest billets occupied by the 3rd Canadian Division, and after staying one night in the village of Divion, where we had our first introduction to Company messing, we finally reached a place called Haillicourt, from where we could hear the guns all day and could see the flares along the front at night—and so the war was getting nearer every minute, or rather we were getting nearer to the war, and strange to tell the nearer we got the better we thought we liked it.

It might be well at this point to state that we were under orders to join the 3rd Canadian Division, and it was generally understood that we were to take the place of the 60th Battalion, which, although the junior Battalion of the 9th Brigade, was held in very high esteem as a fighting unit. The reason given for this most unusual proceeding was that the 60th Battalion, being originally recruited in Quebec, could not get sufficient reinforcements from its own Province, and in consequence was receiving both officers and men from the Province of Ontario. This method of recruiting was evidently frowned upon by superior authority, and the 116th Battalion had been chosen out of many others in England as an alternative to the 60th Battalion, and as a means of overcoming the Provincial question of reinforcements.

Now, as already stated, the 60th had a wonderful record, and individually they were as fine a lot of men as one could meet anywhere; therefore, it is only natural that the news that they were soon to be broken up should cause consternation in the ranks, not only of the 9th Brigade, but the whole of the 3rd Division; and this did not increase the popularity of the 116th.

(As later pointed out by our C.O., we were not only the "baby" battalion of the Canadian Corps, but we were also the "orphan" battalion.)

In addition to our family troubles we were without field kitchens or transport, which made things far from comfortable, and it is certain that during this period our inexperience proved to be our salvation. We were fresh and eager to do credit to the name of our unit and our Commanding Officer (Col. Sharpe), whose untiring energies had succeeded in gaining a place for us in France; so we dealt with our experiences as we found them and passed through them to others.

Whilst at Haillicourt the Battalion was inspected by Major-General Lipsett, G.O.C. 3rd Division, and by Lieut.-General Sir Julian Byng, G.O.C. Canadian Corps,

Beawshott Group (1905)

First Row: Lt. R. C. Henry, M. R. Jacobs, A. W. Baird, F. W. oi, R. J. Blain, W. S. Duncan, J. A. Brewer, W. F. Preston, M. G. and
tree, C. L. S. Newton
Third Row: Lt. H. H. Hyland, Lt. J. J. Dale, Capt. W. E. Shier, Maj. F. H. Moody, Maj. H. P. Cooke, Capt. A. F. Hunt, Maj. G. W.
P. Emery, Capt. A. W. Pratt, Capt. H. V. Gould, Capt. H. L. Major, Capt. G. E. Griffiths
Second Row: Lt. T. W. Hutchison, Lt. G. E. Wells, Capt. J. Munro, M. O., Capt. A. W. McConnell, Adjutant, Maj. R. R. Smith,
Lt. Col. S. S. Sharp, Maj. C. A. W. McCormack, Capt. J. Corbott, Capt. W. C. McFarlane, Capt. N. R. Rathaid, Capt. C. C.
Cowan
Front Row: Lt. C. N. Lennox, Lt. J. H. Hughes, Lt. R. L. Wallace

SOMEWHERE IN FRANCE 17

and after about two weeks' training in the new platoon formation we were moved to Faucquenheim, in order to be closer to the other battalions of the 9th Brigade. The real reason for this move was made obvious during the next few days when orders were received on the 5th March for the Battalion to be split up in the following manner:—

A. Company was to go to the 58th Battalion;
B. Company to the 60th Battalion;
C. Company to the 43rd Battalion;
D. Company to the 52nd Battalion.

The object of this being to give the Battalion training in actual warfare with men who were already experienced in front line work. Further, each Company was split up so that one platoon was apportioned to each Company of the different Battalions as above, and all that now remained of the youthful 116th was an ardent desire to get through the "baptism of fire" with as much glory and as few casualties as possible.

On the 11th March the 9th Brigade, composed of the 43rd, 52nd, 58th and 60th Battalions, moved into the trenches at the foot of Vimy Ridge, accompanied by their unwelcome but willing guests from the 116th. Apart from working parties and general trench routine, which to the inexperienced is all more or less exciting (especially the working parties), nothing of any great military value was accomplished during this tour, and by the 25th of the month our Battalion was reassembled at old friend Houdain, where the experiences of the past fortnight were feverishly discussed and compared. It was generally conceded that trench warfare had not all the advantages the instructors at Bramshott had claimed for it, and that "Take Me Back to Dear Old Blighty" was not such a rotten song after all.

Several of the Companies had encountered mud in the trenches, well over their knees, and, as military overcoats are not constructed for mud wading, a great many of the men in these Companies, following the advice of the "old" soldiers in the Battalions to which they were attached, had cut their coats in accordance, not with orders from the 9th Brigade, but with the depth of the mud encountered. As these tailoring alterations were for the most part made by means of the Service Jack Knife the results were hardly in keeping with (K.R. and O.), and by the look on the C.O.'s face when he inspected the Battalion for the first time after its reassembly at Houdain there was certainly trouble in store for somebody.

The next day saw about 200 brave, but ragged warriors, lined up outside Battalion Orderly Room, awaiting sentence for destroying Government property. The sentences were not severe, but the Battalion tailor had his hands full for a while.

CHAPTER II.

VIMY RIDGE.

OUR sojourn in Houdain was short and sweet. The villagers did everything in their power to make us comfortable, and in return the local *estaminets* were well patronized. The boys of No. 7 platoon who were quartered in a brewery were particularly loath to leave, but a pile of trouble was in store for the Canadians, and it was quite universally known that on the 9th of April the Canadian Corps was to carry out an operation in conjunction with Imperial troops that would result in the immediate departure of the enemy from the summit of Vimy Ridge.

For two years he had looked down into our trenches from the top of that accursed ridge, which had been lost by the French in the early days of the war. He could see the country behind our lines for a distance of about 5 miles, and although every artifice in the dictionary of camouflage had been used to conceal the hundreds of guns which were hauled in, under cover of darkness, for the attack, Mister Fritz could not help seeing something of our preparations. His nerves were certainly on edge, but it was equally certain that he underestimated both the strength and number of our guns and the courage of the assaulting troops.

To drive him from the top of the ridge we must advance a distance of nearly three miles, uphill, over deep mud and shell holes, and through barbed wire entanglements strung across the front in a way that only Germans with a dread of British steel know how to do. Such an advance, even without a shot being fired from his lines, would be quite an undertaking; and so he sat back in his deep dug-outs around the "Zwichen Stellung," and smiled at the idea of anyone taking that comfortable home away from him.

This, then, was the situation when we received orders on the 7th of April to vacate our billets in Houdain and take over a series of mud holes on the top of Mt. St. Eloi, called Dumbell Camp.

From this position, which was right on the edge of a wood (Bois Des Alleux), we had a wonderful view of Vimy Ridge, and also made an equally wonderful target for Fritz's high-velocity gunners, who seemed to suspect, and rightly so, that that wood of ours was a good hiding place for troops. (There must have been at least two Brigades in the vicinity, to say nothing of countless ammunition dumps and big guns.) His shooting was erratic so far as we were concerned, the shells either going over our heads into the Engineers' Camp or falling short amongst the mud holes of another battalion.

And here we stayed until the morning of the 9th of April, which was the day set for the attack. No definite position among the assaulting troops was assigned to us, the whole of the 9th Brigade being in reserve, but we

VIMY RIDGE   21

were told that we would be used to consolidate the captured trenches, and that we might win much honour and glory by conveying ammunition and trench material to the front line, in the event of a successful attack. These little jobs sound rather tame in comparison with honest fighting, but in reality they require just as much skill and courage. Ask any infantry man which he would rather do—go "over the top" or be in reserve and do working parties, and he will choose "going over the top" every time. We had not yet reached the point where we could appreciate these little distinctions, and in consequence were inclined to underestimate the importance of the part allotted to us.

The dawn of the 9th of April, 1917, saw perhaps the fiercest and most scientific artillery barrage of the war (so far) let loose on the German front and support line trenches. Fritz must surely have realized that this was something more than the daily "warm up," which our artillery had been giving him during the last three weeks, and when its full meaning had sunk into his thick and short-cropped head his feelings must have been far from happy.

The boot was to be on the other foot now, for instead of watching us swimming around in the mud of the Souchez Valley, we were soon to see him flying across the lowland which stretches from the eastern side of the Ridge towards Avion and Lens, with the lash of our shells and bullets around his ears.

From our position we could see only the flash of the

guns as it was scarcely daylight, when, like a mighty earthquake, the artillery burst forth, sounding the keynote of the advance to our waiting comrades in the trenches.

Gazing into the smoke and dust, caused by the bursting shells, we vainly tried to picture the drama that had just begun, and many a prayer for success went up from the watchers on Mount St. Eloi that morning.

The attack was evidently progressing, for soon after zero hour, we received orders for one Company to go forward immediately, three platoons to act as carrying parties, and one platoon for wiring in front of some strong points which were to be established by the P.P.C.L.I. The order in which our Companies would be used had been previously decided by ballot, for it goes without saying that all four Companies were anxious to be first—"B" Company were the lucky ones, and under Major Moody, moved out accompanied by a detachment of Engineers under whose supervision the defences of the strong points would be constructed. "A" Company (Major Cooke), "C" Company (Major Currie), and "D" Company (Major Bird) moved out later in the day.

The work by these Companies, acting independently for the first time, deserves the highest praise, and their adventures throughout that memorable day would almost fill a book in themselves. The Sector of the ridge where our Companies were employed had been cleared of the enemy and by the time that No. 8 platoon had reached

VIMY RIDGE 23

the new front line around La Folie Farm, the German artillerymen, who up till now had been chiefly engaged in dragging their guns to safety, were searching the top of the ridge in an endeavour to retard the work of consolidation. They must have sighted No. 8 platoon, for no sooner had our men begun work on the wiring schemes than a veritable hail of shells was poured into them. In spite of heavy casualties the work of consolidation was continued and completed, and towards midnight all companies reported in to Dumbell Camp, having lost ten men killed and thirty wounded, including Company Sergeant Major Graves.

The reports from all parts of the line fulfilled the highest expectations, and the prisoners' cages were crowded beyond capacity, but for the next few days there was to be no rest for anyone until our new line had been so firmly established as to admit of no possibility for a successful counter-attack by the Bosch.

The following day the Battalion furnished parties to assist in the general work of consolidation, and at about 5 o'clock in the evening, orders were received for us to take over the front line from the 8th Brigade, composed of the 1st, 2nd, 4th and 5th Battalions, C.M.R. It looked as if we might get into some of the fighting after all, and with very mixed feelings the inevitable advance party, consisting of 1 officer and 1 N.C.O. from each Company and H.Q., started out in the direction of a certain map location called "Spandau Haus" where the C.M.R. Battalions had established their headquarters.

The line of march brought us through territory already well known—Berthonval Farm, La Targette Corners, Goodman Tunnel, Chassery Crater, etc., and further on, through territory fresh with the smell of the Bosch.

It is a very curious sensation to walk boldly across the shell holes, which only recently were called "No Man's Land," and over which we had been wont to crawl about with our noses pretty close to the ground. By the time we reached Spandau Haus, night had set in, and to look over the line with any intelligence would be an impossibility. This must have been a very joyous relief to the C.M.R.'s, for they were all dog tired, and to have to more or less instruct a new Battalion in all the intricacies of a newly captured position was asking them a little too much after their experiences of the last 36 hours. This is evidently what Divisional Headquarters thought too, for by the time our party had returned to Dumbell Camp, having carefully marked on their maps all the information possible, it was announced that the relief of the 8th Brigade by our Battalion had been cancelled, and that the 60th Battalion would go forward in our place—shouts of joy, especially by the advance party, who had done ten miles in the pouring rain. Instead, therefore, of holding Vimy Ridge against the now infuriated Bosch, we were reduced to taking over the support trenches soon to be vacated by the 60th, and at dusk the following day, during a heavy fall of snow, these changes were successfully carried out. The Battalion was shelled heavily by 5.9's just as it reached

The Original "Orderly Room Staff"

VIMY RIDGE 25

the old crater line, and had several casualties, including Lt. John Doble, who was killed.

During the next ten days the whole Battalion was engaged in the reconstruction of the Lens-Arras road, between Thélus and Vimy, which had been rendered practically impassable by the recent barrages. This work was both laborious and nerve-racking. Fritz was quite aware that the road was one of our only lines of communication, having used it himself, and consequently he was not going to let us put it into good condition for nothing. Every variety of "hate," large and small, and generally in series of four, was thrown at that road blocked with mule transport, guns, ambulances, and working parties (chiefly 116th Battalion)? and it is the most extraordinary thing that the work of reconstruction progressed as favorably as it did, and that there were not more casualties.

During this period opportunities were afforded us for looking over the Corps front from the top of the ridge, and for admiring the recent work of our own artillery on the German defences. Whilst reconnoitring the forward positions Lt. W. K. Kift and Lt. H. L. Major both received wounds from which they afterwards died. The laborious work of road-making with its daily toll of casualties continued, until one day, a note from Battalion Headquarters announced that we would not become a fighting unit as heretofore decided, but that we would be made into a pioneer battalion and be attached permanently to the 8th Brigade. All this in the interest of the Corps, etc., etc., etc. We were still "chewing the rag" over this latest development when along came the Colonel himself to announce that all previous orders regarding pioneer battalions had been cancelled, and that it had been definitely decided for us to take over the 60th Battalion. In order to do this with the least confusion possible, we were to be moved back to the Berthonval Farm area, where Fritz's shells were not likely to disturb us, all of which prophecies excepting the one concerning the shells came true.

CHAPTER III.

Umpty Umps.

THE successful capture of Vimy Ridge ended another chapter in the annals of the Canadian Corps which was soon to be regarded as second to none on the Western front. It also witnessed the birth of a new battalion, whose fame up to the present, had not extended beyond the borders of the County of Ontario, but whose ideals, if lived up to, would make it second to none in the gallant Corps to which it now belonged.

The recent successes had not been achieved without heavy casualties, and when these casualties were made good by reinforcements it was quite evident that the other Battalions in our Division were not greatly superior to our own in the way of old and experienced soldiers. Their Headquarters were, of course, composed of men who had seen considerable fighting, but otherwise from now on we were all more or less on an equal footing.

The months of May and June slipped away, with nothing more important being allotted to us than taking over a line of trenches and holding them; in fact, the usual trench routine with working parties mixed in. As a special treat one night we were allowed to dig a jumping-off trench for another Battalion, who were conducting a raid in our Sector; but anything in the nature of real fighting was considered beyond us for the present, although there was a certain amount going on practically all the time, the Bosch being pushed gently but firmly away from the Ridge as far as Avion and Méricourt— a distance of four miles.

In these minor operations, as they were called, the 116th was either detailed as the supporting Battalion or else the reserve Battalion for the Brigade, and as the Bosch showed very little inclination to remain in his then exposed positions, the result was that by the middle of July the "Umpty Umps" (as we had been nicknamed, not wholly in fun, by the older units) had not been actually engaged in any action of a direct nature whatsoever. In spite of this, our casualties had been quite heavy, indicating that the main line of resistance is not always the healthiest place to occupy during an engagement; in fact, with the exception of Major Currie, "C" Company, not one of our original Company Commanders remained. During one of these tours in the line one of our companies came across a memorial to the 60th Battalion erected by some of their men close to the Village of Vimy. The memorial was in the shape of a cross with the inscription "In memory of the 60th Battalion. 1915—Raised by Patriotism. 1917—Killed by Politics." A reflection perhaps not entirely without foundation.

On the 5th of July the 9th Brigade was withdrawn to Divisional reserve at Chateau de la Haie—meaning that for a week at least we would have no working parties, also that we would all get an opportunity of having a real live shower bath and a change of underclothes, which in most cases was an urgent necessity.

It was during this period that the Brigade Commander announced his intention of formally inspecting us, and at the completion of his inspection, having congratulated us on our good appearance and also our general behaviour since joining his Brigade, he pointed out that although we had shown extraordinary ability at baseball and other sports, having lately won the Brigade Championship, much to the discomfiture of the older Battalions, we had not so far proved our ability in the noblest sport of all, namely, that of "strafing the Hun." Proceeding, he indicated that we would be given every opportunity to do this during the next tour of the Brigade in the line. This announcement was greeted by "prolonged cheering," for there was nothing to our minds so alluring as the anticipation of getting to grips with an enemy who had inflicted casualties amongst us, and upon whom we had had no opportunity for retaliation.

Great was the excitement after the departure of the Brigadier, and many the conjectures as to the nature of the "opportunity" we had so long been waiting for; even the visit of King George V., for whom we lined the road that afternoon, did little or nothing in removing the one thought that was uppermost in the mind of each one of us.

Having no scheme of our own, it was evidently the

duty of Divisional or Brigade H.Q. to devise some scheme for us, and this they were not long in doing, for on the 12th of July—four days after the visit of the Brigadier—we received orders that instead of proceeding up the line with the rest of the Brigade we would occupy Comak Camp in the neighborhood of Berthonval Farm and there carry out practices over taped trenches for a raid, the details of which would be disclosed to us later.

CHAPTER IV.

THE RAID.

JUST to the south of the Village of Avion there is situated a colliery called Fossé 4, with its necessary attendant, a large and ugly slag heap, shaped like a truncated cone. If our front line, at that time, might be considered as a line running due east and west and just to the south of Avion, then Fossé 4 was almost entirely within the German lines, with just the southern fringe of the slag heap extending into "No Man's Land."

The German front line, so far as this account is concerned, extended round the base of the slag heap and then south-east, where it joined a system of trenches known as the Méricourt Maze at about two hundred and fifty yards distance.

About 300 yards behind the German front line and running parallel to it was a railway embankment, scarcely less than 24 feet in height; and about midway between the German lines and our own and parallel to our line was a road (Quebec Road). Scatter around a few rows of ruined houses, a garden fence, and a couple of brick piles and you will have what the 3rd Divisional Staff considered to be an ideal location for a raid.

THE 116TH BATTALION IN FRANCE

The slag heap was reported to be a veritable nest of machine guns, and trench mortars; the railway embankment was believed to be fairly honeycombed with dug-outs, but all that was actually and really known was that the German front line was strongly barricaded and full of Germans, and that Quebec Road was partly sunken and full of wire. The place and opportunity having therefore been supplied it remained for us to fix the time and arrange the details.

Immediately upon arrival at Comak Camp a stretch of ground was selected for practice, and the Engineers who started at once to work on the taped trenches, made such good progress that the following morning everything was in readiness for our first trial. In the meantime a plan of attack was formulated, of which the following is a brief résumé: "A" Company (Capt. Gould) would capture and hold the German front line (known as Metal Trench) looking after any machine guns and trench mortar posts found on the slag heap, together with all dug-outs in the neighborhood.

"B" Company (Capt. Allen) on the left, and "C" Company (Major Currie) on the right would pass through "A" Company continuing on to the railway embankment, which they would proceed to capture, destroying all dug-outs and M.G. emplacements. Upon a given signal from Battalion Headquarters raiding Companies would retire, protected by covering parties left along the railway embankment and communication trenches, "A" Company to remain in Metal Trench until all of "B"

The Battalion Band

THE RAID 33

and "C" Companies had withdrawn. The most unpleasant job of all, perhaps, that of holding the Battalion front during the raid, was assigned to "D" Company (Capt. Ritchie).

The attack was to be carried out at night (1 a.m.) and under cover of an artillery and M.G. Barrage.

For the next few days the one topic of conversation was the raid, and at least two practices a day were carried out over the taped trenches, until we considered ourselves perfect enough to invite the Divisional and Brigade Commanders to attend our final practice before going into the line. This they did and pronounced themselves well satisfied.

During these preparations our Commanding Officer, Col. S. Sharpe, was untiring in his energies towards overcoming the numerous difficulties that so frequently presented themselves, and he personally led a reconnoitring party into Avion in broad daylight, which enabled us to overlook the territory to be raided from the second story of a ruined house.

On the 18th of July we received orders to move into the line and to take over the trenches occupied by the 5th C.M.R. At dusk that evening the Battalion assembled, and after wishing God-speed to Major Cameron, our Second in Command, who was leaving that night for Canada, a most stirring and eloquent address was made by Col. Sharpe; so that when we moved off by Companies in the direction of Vimy Ridge, to the strains of "John Peel," the regimental march, there was scarcely a more confident lot of men in the whole Allied Army.

At about 9.30 p.m., on the 22nd July, a start was made to assemble the raiding Companies behind Quebec Road, which was the jumping-off position for the raid. Each man was equipped with an electric torch-light for use in the German lines, and a large white patch was sewn on the front of everybody's box respirator, which was thought to be a good means of identification in the dark. About midnight, therefore, the platoons were being led quietly and stealthily into position. Suddenly the bells in the German trenches, not a hundred yards from the right flank, began to ring; gas fumes were rapidly making their way over our positions. It was difficult to tell whether the gas was merely lachrymatory or poisonous, and at the first indication every officer and man had slipped on his gas helmet.

It is hard enough to find your way about in the dark under ordinary conditions, but with a gas helmet on it is absolutely impossible, and in less time than it takes to tell, the greatest confusion arose, and the success of the whole operation hung in the balance. A desperate situation confronted the Battalion; in a little while our artillery barrage would open, and its programme would be carried out while our men were stumbling blindly through the gas fumes, and in due course the enemy artillery would open up in retaliation, and our men, helpless with their gas helmets on, would be wiped out without a chance for their lives. For about thirty minutes the situation was critical and fraught with the greatest difficulties; the darkness, the gas, the fumes, the irregularities of the ground, wire entanglements, ruins, shell holes, all combined to make the assembling of our companies slow and difficult.

Chances had to be taken, and gas helmets were removed, the mouthpiece alone being used, and in this manner, our eyes streaming with tears and nerves strung to the highest pitch, we eventually reached our positions around the Quebec Road about five minutes before zero hour.

Exactly on the stroke of one the barrage opened, falling like a hailstorm on the German front line, which was lit up along its entire length by the bursting shells. It was certainly an unmerciful pounding and seemed to fill us with an ardent desire to get over there, and like Julius Caesar, "negotium finire."

As the barrage opened "A" Company crept across the Quebec Road through the lanes in the wire which had been previously cut by the scouts, and at zero, plus three minutes, at which moment the barrage lifted off Metal Trench to the Railway embankment, they rushed forward, closely followed by "B" Company on the left and "C" Company on the right. By the time "A" Company reached Metal Trench the Huns had begun to pour out of their dug-outs in which they had taken refuge during the shell storm, and hand-to-hand fighting ensued, in which many of the enemy were either killed or taken prisoners; leaving "A" Company to deal with the destruction of the dug-outs and the capture of the slag heap, as previously arranged, "B" and "C" Companies proceeded to the final objective.

As already anticipated, our greatest trouble was to be from the flanks, and during the final stages of the attack, in which "B" and "C" Companies rushed the embankment, capturing many prisoners, some enemy machine guns came into action and inflicted heavy casualties on us. In spite of this, everything seemed to be happening just in the way we had practised it at Berthonval Farm, even the special carrying parties that were to bring up trench mats for crossing the wire believed to exist around the embankment, arrived, and were much disappointed when they were told they would not be needed. Also the signallers specially attached to Companies for communication with Battalion Headquarters came through, but were unable to use their lamps on account of the smoke and gas.

Considerable trouble was experienced with refractory prisoners, and the evacuation of our casualties was a matter of the greatest difficulty, since by the time "B" and "C" Companies had reached the embankment all sense of direction was lost on account of the darkness and gas fumes, which were now blowing back over the German lines.

The work of destruction completed, the two Companies, "B" and "C", withdrew as best they could, covered by sections, one from each platoon, acting as a rear-guard.

Observation posts were left on the Railway Embankment at each flank with supporting posts behind them, "A" Company remaining in Metal Trench until "B" and "C" Companies had completed their withdrawal. The observation posts were chiefly organized by Lt. Lennox of "B" Company and Lt. Neil of "C" Company, who were in command of the flank platoons.

"D" Company had detailed parties under Lt. Weber and Lt. Lick, which were to relieve at daybreak the posts left respectively by "B" and "C" Companies. Lt. Lick was, however, killed by a shell near Metal Trench, and his sergeant and corporal wounded. Lt. Weber went up on the left and reached Metal Trench, but at 4.45 a.m. the Germans had counter-attacked in force and our posts withdrew fighting as ordered. When it was learned that Lt. Neil and Lt. Lick were killed and that Lt. Lennox and Lt. Weber were missing a party was sent up Meander Trench to assist the posts. This party got out between Metal Trench and the Railway Embankment just as the Germans began to swarm over it, and also attack from the flank. Our party was obliged to withdraw, taking the balance of the men on the posts with it. Stiff fighting took place all the way back, and many of the enemy were killed.

In such an operation it would be very difficult and most unfair to mention the work of any one particular platoon, section, or man, since all we had planned to do was done, and this in the face of many serious handicaps. The care of our wounded was now the first consideration, and Capt. Moore, with his staff, who had established an advance Regimental Aid Post (later known as "Moore's Aid Post") at the junction of the Lens-Arras Railway and the Avion Road, were busy until daylight, when a German observation balloon caught sight of them, and they were forced by heavy shell fire to retire to a more protected position.

And so it was only through the co-operation and courage of all ranks that we had at last won the right to our place in the 9th Brigade and the Canadian Corps. Let it be said that this was only one of a great many successful raids carried out by Canadian troops, and which made them famous on all the Western front.

In sum we had captured 60 prisoners, including two officers, and killed at least twice that number, our own casualties being five officers—Lts. V. C. Lick, C. S. Lennox, F. S. Neil, T. W. Hutchison, G. R. Weber—and twenty-five other ranks killed, three officers and forty-two other ranks wounded.

It might be of interest to compare the two communiqués published shortly afterwards:

GERMAN—Strong enemy thrusts in the neighborhood of Avion easily repulsed with heavy casualties.

BRITISH—Early this morning our troops carried out a minor enterprise S.E. of Avion. The first objective was easily captured, but heavy fighting ensued at the railway embankment. After a severe struggle the whole of the German garrison was either killed or captured and all their dug-outs were destroyed—about fifty—sixty Ger-

THE RAID 39

mans are reported to have been taken. Our total casualties are believed to be about the same as the number of German prisoners. The enemy's losses were heavy.

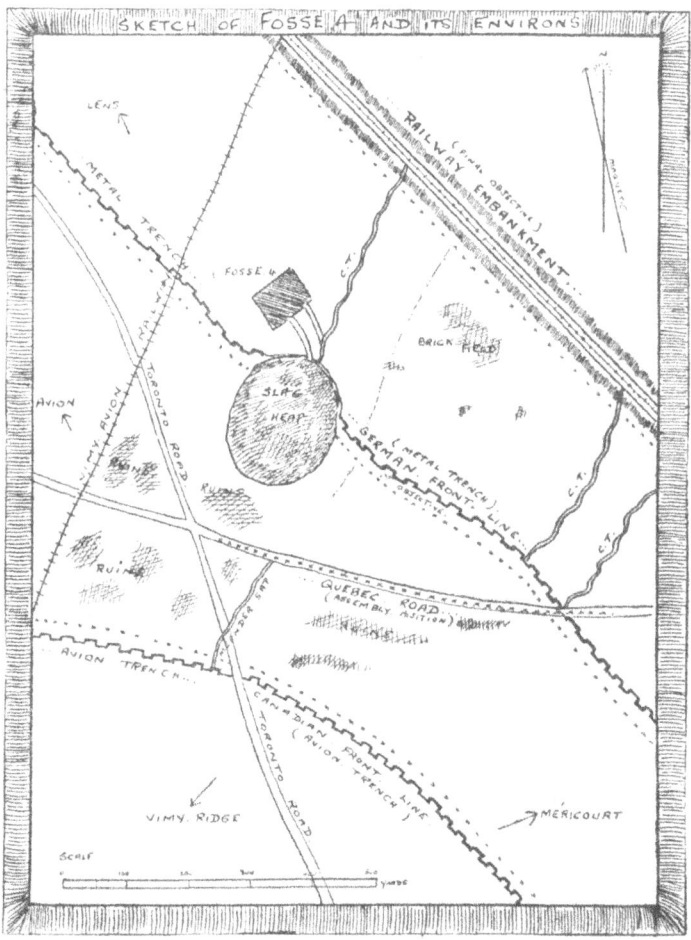

CHAPTER V.

HILL SEVENTY.

EVERY little while, but generally at intervals of about four months, it fell to the lot of each division to be withdrawn entirely from the line for the purpose of rest and reorganization.

After a long tour of trench duty, during which life at its best is merely an existence, it can be readily appreciated that these periods of rest were greatly looked forward to by all ranks.

Each Corps had a specified rest area, generally from 12 to 14 miles behind the line, and when a division came out, a village in that area was allotted to each battalion or sometimes one village to two battalions. There were, of course, the good villages and the bad villages, and for about a week before going out there was always a good deal of speculation as to which village the battalion would go to. At the beginning of August, the 3rd Canadian Division was withdrawn from the line, and it fell to our lot to get the Village of Auchel, conceded by many to be the Queen of billets in the Corps area; but unfortunately for us we did not arrive there until about the 15th of the month, being held up at Camblain L'Abbée (Corps Headquarters) on account of manoeuvres. Open fighting had suddenly become all the rage, probably in anticipation of the drive the following August, and

GROUP OF N.C.O.'S TAKEN AT NIAGARA, 1916

R.S.M. F. H. HINDLE
(Awarded D.C.M. for bravery
in the Field)

"QUARTERS" McKAY
(Awarded the Meritorious Service Medal for continuous gallant service with the Battalion throughout its Campaign in France)

HILL SEVENTY 41

our whole division took part in extensive practices. At about this time No. 1 Platoon under Lt. Ott, distinguished itself in a Corps rifle competition, held at Ferfay, winning first place in the Division and only losing first place in the Corps through a technicality.

Considering the representative gathering, which included units such as the R.C.R. and P.P.C.L.I., the victory reflects the greatest credit upon the spirit and training of our platoon.

At the completion of the manoeuvres we moved to Auchel and for a week lived like human beings again, almost forgetting that there was a war going on, and we had just begun to settle down to a gay village life when we were rushed unceremoniously to the north of Lens to relieve certain units of the 2nd Canadian Division, who were engaged in a scrap which was afterwards known as the Battle of Hill Seventy. And so, on August 20th, amid the cries of "Bonne chance" from our friends in Auchel, we marched away with considerable reluctance, arriving the same evening at Gouy Servins, which was a reminder of the early days of the Battalion in France. Even then some of us had marched in high spirits from Auchel to Gouy Servins on a first visit to the trenches; and Gouy Servins at that time was everything that the first part of its name would imply. To-day however, in the middle of an almost perfect summer, so far as weather was concerned, the roads were hard and dusty and the enthusiasm to reach the front line perhaps not quite so apparent.

Having rested over-night, the march was continued, until about noon we reached Sains-en-Gohelle, another curiously descriptive name, but more commonly known as Fossé 10, which forms part of a chain of mining villages in the neighborhood of Lens.

Things seemed to be quite lively around these parts and high-velocity shells were dropping almost too close to make a quiet meal possible. Fossé 10 was really a staging camp to the front line, and there was naturally considerable confusion due to the relief that was in progress between the 2nd and 3rd Canadian Divisions.

Before very long orders were received that the 116th Battalion would relieve the 27th Battalion that night. A reconnoitring party consisting of the C.O., the company commanders of "A" and "D" Companies who were to take over the front line, the scout officer and the M.O. set off early in the afternoon, as it was fully realized that a ticklish relief was in store for us.

From information received it was understood that the 2nd Division had attacked at daybreak and had made splendid progress, but that owing to the difficulties of communication, due to intense artillery fire, the situation, and in particular the line established by the 27th Battalion, was decidedly obscure.

It was whilst this party was making its way forward to the village of Cité St. Pierre that Captain James Moore, our gallant and popular M.O., and two of the chief members of his staff were severely wounded.

During the remainder of the day and early part of

the night the Bosch artillery was more than usually aggressive, in retaliation no doubt for their recent losses, in fact the R.S.M. of the 27th Battalion remarked that the artillery concentration on such a small frontage was heavier than our troops had experienced at any time during the Somme offensive, an interesting comparison although not entirely appreciated by us at that time.

Under such conditions the details of the relief are best left to the imagination. To cut a horrible nightmare short it may be said that towards 3 a.m. the following morning a line was established by our men in badly demolished trenches and shell holes running through a portion of the ruined Cité St. Elizabeth to the outskirts of the City of Lens proper. Our final dispositions were in the front line right sector "D" Company (Captain Pratt), left sector "A" Company (Captain Ritchie). In close support "C" Company (Major Currie), in reserve "B" Company (Captain Every). The support and reserve companies both occupied whatever ruins or cellars they could find.

This was a truly delightful awakening after our recent rest in billets!

The enemy was either very nervous or else he suspected that a relief was in progress, for during the next forty-eight hours, we were treated to every variety of explosive, both large and high.

So intense was the fire from his artillery, that our front line companies experienced considerable difficulty in carrying out the all-important work of consolidation;

whilst the support and reserve companies were equally handicapped in their work of establishing ammunition dumps, and providing burial and ration parties.

After twelve days, during which we spent eight in the front line and suffered casualties of no less than twenty O.R's. killed and two officers and ninety O.R's. wounded, we were more than glad to be relieved by the 15th Battalion (1st Division).

After spending one night at Marqueffles Farm, in the neighborhood of Boulay Grenay, we marched south to our old familiar front around Vimy Ridge, taking over from the 11th Battalion East Lancashire Regiment, who were in reserve along the Arras-Avion railway embankment. The dug-out accommodation, having been constructed by the Bosch, was excellent, if somewhat dirty, and with the exception of one or two working parties we had nothing very much to worry us. Now and again Fritz would take it into his head to land a few salvos into the artillery positions in Vimy Village, about 300 yards away, and as we had to go there for water it was generally advisable to time our visits so as not to coincide with the arrival of his shells. He used to fool us sometimes though, and then the water party would return rather hurriedly, minus the water and the petrol tins for carrying it.

On the 15th September we relieved the 58th Battalion in the front line (Totnes Trench), situated in front of Méricourt, at an average distance of fifteen hundred yards from the Bosch front line. The 58th informed us

The Distinguished
Conduct Medal
Number won by Batt.
27

The Meritorious
Service Medal
Number won by Batt.
7

The Distinguished
Service Order
Number won by Batt.
7

The Military Medal
Number won by Batt.
102

The Military Cross
Number won by Batt.
26

HILL SEVENTY 45

that they had had an ideal tour with scarcely any shelling, but that during their last day in, the Bosch had registered several times with 5.9's on the right sector, now occupied by our "B" Company. This information was rather disconcerting, especially for the posts in that neighborhood. Anyway, a strict watch was established by the lookouts, and on the evening of the 16th, Company Commanders were called hurriedly to a conference at Battalion Headquarters. Information was that small parties of German officers had been seen that day with maps pointing in the direction of our trenches, and that messages had been intercepted indicating the possibility of a raid on our line that night. In consequence every precaution was taken and the battle patrols, which were in the habit of scouring "No Man's Land" each evening, were held in the front line.

It was indeed a timely warning, for at 3 a.m., precisely, on the 17th, an almost perfect barrage dropped on our front line and supports. Now a certain Army order stating that no S.O.S. must be sent up until it was absolutely assured that the enemy was attacking had been recently impressed on us, and that is probably the reason why only one Company put one up (Red over Red over Red). Our artillery were sound asleep, for they never responded at all. The barrage lifted off our front line and it was evident that we were "for it."

Up went another S.O.S., but our artillery still slept on. A few of the enemy crept through the wire and entered "C" Company's frontage in an empty bay at its junction with 12th Ave. communication trench. They left the trench immediately, having captured Pte. Dewes of "B" Company, who had been wounded by the barrage, and was evidently on his way out to the rear. The smoke and dust were so thick we could see nothing, and a continuous rifle and Lewis gun fire was our only means of retaliation.

About daybreak we captured two of the enemy who had become entangled in our wire; unfortunately one of them refused to surrender and was shot dead by Lewis gunners before we could get him in. Our prisoner informed us that a large raid had been intended, and that the attacking party (seventy-three in number) was composed of "Stürm Trüppen" (storm troops) who had been rushed up to the line that night in automobiles especially for this little entertainment. He also presented us with the photo of his company—published in this book. In evidence of what our prisoner told us we later found several mobile charges in front of our wire intended no doubt for the destruction of the dug-outs, of which we had none, and whole piles of stick and egg bombs, which came in very handy as souvenirs for the troops.

On the evening of the 18th, the battalion was relieved by the Royal Canadian Regiment (Fritz had timed his raid just 24 hours too soon!!) and marched to Thélus Caves, from where we were transported by light railway to Fraser Camp (Mount St. Eloi), arriving there about dawn.

HILL SEVENTY 47

For purposes of comparison later on, let it be said that the total casualties of the battalion up to the present time, or for seven months' active service, numbered eighteen officers and two hundred and seventy other ranks killed, wounded and missing.

Practically the whole of these memoirs so far has been devoted to the personnel of the battalion actually doing duty in the trenches, and no mention has been made of the work done by the Quartermaster's department and the transport section.

Whenever the battalion moved into the line the transport and Quartermaster's stores remained behind together with what was known as Rear Battalion Headquarters, and they were jointly responsible for supplying to the battalion each day, food, clothes, ammunition, rum, etc., in fact all the necessaries of life, and all the necessaries of war so far as the infantry soldier is concerned, including mail and reinforcements.

The men belonging to these sections did not therefore come actually into contact with the enemy, as was the case with the men in the trenches, but their duties were none the less arduous and none the less dangerous. Every night rations must be carried to the battalion in the line, and the roads and pathways along which the transport must travel were nearly always swept by machine gun and artillery fire, and the transport lines themselves came in for quite a little shelling by the German heavies.

Our transport section and Q.M. department had

never let us down so far, which speaks very highly for their personnel, and that they never came into direct contact with the enemy is not strictly accurate, since a few days after arriving at Fraser Camp our Quartermaster, who was riding towards La Targette Corners, was chased by an enemy plane. His own description of his feelings when he realized the relative speed of his horse on the gallop and the German plane, is beyond words, and after a minute or so of terrible suspense, during which the German plane was putting machine gun groups all round him, he decided that the duel was unfair and promptly rolled off his horse into the ditch. The German airman flew home in triumph.

On the 30th September Divine Service for the whole Brigade was held in the fields around Berthonval Farm, and afterwards an investiture. The Corps, Divisional and Brigade Commanders were present and the Corps Commander personally decorated a number of our N.C.O's. and men who had distinguished themselves in the raid of July 23rd. The proceedings were slightly marred by the activities of a German aeroplane, which seemed to be drawing the fire of every "Archie" in the neighborhood, with the result that nose caps were flying around and greatly disturbing the steadiness of the troops.

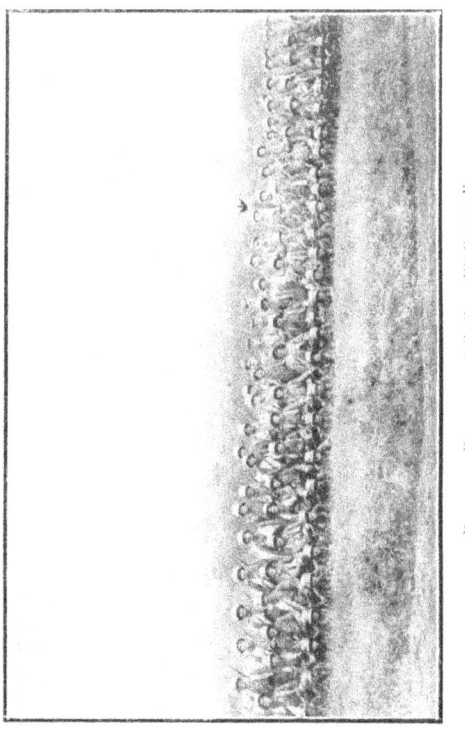

Raiding Party of "Sturm Truppen"
Photo taken from prisoner.

CHAPTER VI.

PASSCHENDAELE.

WE had not been in Fraser Camp for more than two days when we were invited to pay a visit to some taped trenches close to Villers au Bois, and maps of the area which they represented were freely distributed.

The successful capture of Vimy Ridge had certainly improved our position considerably, but there was still a decided salient round the city of Lens, which seemed to create a certain amount of uneasiness among the H.Q. staff. To straighten out this salient was therefore the object now in view, and to this end the entire Canadian Corps was to be engaged. An assault through Avion and Méricourt, which were situated to the south of Lens, combined with a strong demonstration north of that city, was the plan of campaign to be adopted, the result of which, if successful, would not only straighten the existing salient, but would force the Germans to evacuate Lens itself.

Tanks were to be used in conjunction with the infantry, and in order to become acquainted with their peculiarities we attended a demonstration by the Tank Corps at Mailly, which was most instructive. For two solid weeks we worked hard on this scheme, practising over the taped trenches every day, and then suddenly the practices ceased, and strawberry jam was substituted for the everlasting plum and apple. This generally meant that the time for the attack was drawing near, but in this case it did not materialize, for on the 14th of October we received orders to move on the next day to Ourton and to entrain for Godewaersvelde, in Belgium. This change of tactics, quite unforeseen, was not unpopular with us, as we had not yet seen Belgium, and never having been there, we thought we might like it, and this in spite of many prophecies to the contrary.

After a very long and tedious train journey we arrived at our destination and marched to billets in Caestre. After resting here for two days and surprising the natives with our fondness for corn on the cob, which until now they had used entirely as cattle fodder, we were informed of the reason for our enforced presence in this district.

Operations in front of Ypres had reached a deadlock. The troops engaged, consisting chiefly of Australians and New Zealanders, had advanced nearly three miles under conditions that must have been almost heartbreaking. It had poured with rain every day; the mud was well over their knees, and they were enfiladed from both sides by the German artillery, until finally, they were brought to a halt on the top of Abraham Heights through sheer exhaustion and heavy casualties.

The German defences on this front consisted chiefly of "Pill Boxes"—oblong, concrete constructions, made out of Portland cement (?) and divided into several compartments with small, narrow entrances either at the side or back.

The average head protection in one of these was from four to five feet of solid concrete, and our field artillery shells would bounce off them like tennis balls off the sidewalk.

As soon as the shelling ceased, out would come "Mr. Bosch" with his machine guns, and from selected positions play havoc amongst our troops, floundering around in the mud. Once in a while a twelve-inch "how." would make a direct hit on one of these hornets' nests and then, of course, Fritz would stay in there never to come out again. But a twenty-five-foot target at a range of ten miles is a difficult one to hit, and the majority of the "pill boxes" were captured by hand-to-hand fighting.

The ground seemed to be composed of an endless series of ridges, and you no sooner reached the top of one ridge than another more formidable loomed up in front.

From Abraham Heights the Bellevue Spur (another name for a ridge) dotted here and there with "pill boxes," stood out like a sentinel keeping watch over the village of Passchendaele in the distance, and it was plain to all around that fresh and experienced troops would be needed at this point to effect its capture. There was perhaps no Corps on the Western front at that time more capable of undertaking this difficult task, or as numerically strong, as the Canadian Corps, and that is the reason we ate corn at Caestre instead of hunting the Hun around Lens.

Two more days' rest were given us to digest this news, and to enable parties to visit the area of desolation and gloom which was to be the scene of our future endeavours. Orders were then received to entrain for Ypres, and our arrival at that historic ruin was greeted by many cheers from the outgoing Australian units. From all they told us or rather shouted at us as they crowded into the train we had just left, we began to realize that we were not going to enjoy ourselves quite so much as we thought. "Go to it, yer blighters," they yelled, and away we went. Having occupied several "Camps" in the neighborhood of Wieltje, the 9th Brigade, with the 116th Battalion in support, attacked the Bellevue Spur on the morning of October 26th, and by the morning of the 27th, after one of the fiercest and most bloody onslaughts in its history, succeeded in destroying the entire German garrison.

On the evening of the 27th the 116th Battalion took over the front line from the remnants of the Brigade, remaining there until relieved by the 49th Battalion (7th Brigade)—during the early hours of the 29th October.

We were not sorry to move away from our present gruesome surroundings; but it was not until the 7th November that we actually said "good-bye" to them, as we thought, and moved by bus to Vlamertinghe, and from there to the Watou area, east of Poperinghe, having lost forty-two other ranks killed, three officers and one hundred and one other ranks wounded, and twelve other ranks gassed.

The "Rough Road" to Passchendaele, 1917. (Canadian Official Copyright)

CHAPTER VII.

Rest Billets.

THE general feeling amongst the troops was that they had seen enough of the Ypres salient, or what remained of it, to last them until the end of the war, and as a few "leaves" to Blighty were filtering through there were some lucky ones who had their wish fulfilled. The remainder, however, were sadly deluded, and after billeting in tents for five days found themselves on the way back to that same quagmire they had so earnestly desired never to set eyes on again. This tour of duty, however, proved to be light in comparison with past experiences, and after six days spent in working parties we were finally relieved in Brigade reserve by the Royal Irish Rifles, and on the 19th of November moved by bus to Haverskerque, where we spent the night.

From Haverskerque we marched by easy stages to Bailleul-les-Pernes, probably the poorest village for billets in the neighborhood, but thankful to be alive, and pleased at the prospect of spending the next three weeks anywhere except around Ypres, we settled down to what we considered a much needed rest.

We had great difficulty in securing a parade ground within easy marching distance of, and large enough to accommodate all four Companies, much to the disgust of the C.O., who was never happier than when he could get the Battalion together again after the disintegration entailed by a tour in the line.

The billets were certainly poor, and after parade hours, those who were energetic enough would either wander off to Auchel to renew old acquaintances or else go to Ferfay to see the latest Dumbell Concert Party. There was also a small village called Pernes, about three kilometres away, which most of the boys will remember. "D" Company Officers' mess gave a party there during which a young calf was driven into the dining room of the Café. Somebody at once conceived the idea that calf-riding would be good for the digestion, and there was lots of fun trying to ride the calf, who resented this treatment by throwing each of his would-be riders to the floor. Eventually a long-legged officer from "B" Company succeeded in riding once round the Café, which broke the calf's spirit completely, and he rolled over breathless on his back. The orchestra immediately struck up the "Toreador Song" from Carmen, and the party broke up amidst scenes of the greatest excitement.

During our rest in this village we were given the opportunity to cast our votes for or against Conscription in Canada. The polling was organized by Companies, each Company Orderly Room being temporarily converted into a polling booth. A muster parade was then called, and the whole affair completed in a few hours. It would be quite safe to estimate the result at 99.9%

in favor of conscription, and it seems a pity that all elections and things of the kind, including referendums, cannot be organized in a similar manner.

On November 24th, Major A. W. McConnell, who succeeded Major Cameron as 2nd in command of the battalion, was recalled to Canada, and the vacancy thus caused was filled by Major G. R. Pearkes, M.C., of the 5th C.M.R., who received his appointment through special recommendation of the Divisional Commander.

After spending a quiet and peaceful month at Bailleul-les-Pernes we finally relieved the 9th Sherwood Foresters and the 8th Northumberland Fusiliers in the front line just north of Lens, on the 22nd December, with the pleasant prospect of being there for Christmas Day.

About this time Col. S. Sharpe proceeded to England for the Senior Officers' Staff Course, and during his absence Major G. R. Pearkes assumed command of the battalion. Although Christmas Day was spent in feasting chiefly on "Bully," on the night of the 26th December warning was received of an intended raid by the Germans, and a raid was actually made on Sap 6 at 6.30 a.m. the following morning, but the enemy was successfully driven off.

The condition of the trenches in this sector was the worst imaginable. The mud was not only knee deep but like glue, and it was not at all an unusual occurrence for a man to lose his boots and socks in his endeavours to extricate himself. One of the smallest of our officers, Capt. Hughes, was heard to remark that it was a good thing for him that his colors were painted on his helmet. On one memorable occasion we were relieving the 58th Battalion—the bad conditions had been rendered even worse by a heavy fall of snow. Our relieving companies became so exhausted, which is not to be wondered at when one remembers the unmercifully heavy equipment usually carried into the line, that the relief which should have been completed about 10 p.m. was not actually reported until 3 a.m. the following morning. Even when the 58th had been relieved they found it impossible to get out until daylight.

The chief work of the period was the reorganization of the front line and the building of strong points. On the 22nd January, 1918, at 5.40 p.m., the enemy raided No. 4 post, but his party was caught in a barrage and obliged to retire. The conduct of Corporal Allen in the handling of his section was most exemplary. Several important patrols were made during which Lieutenant F. A. McGrotty received wounds from which he afterwards died.

Towards the end of February the battalion moved back to its old familiar hunting ground around Avion, where, although the trenches and general conditions were excellent, we sustained a series of misfortunes. Patrols went out every night through the ruins of Avion to try and locate enemy posts and whilst engaged in this work we lost two of our officers, Lieutenant C. R. Hillis and Lieutenant R. W. Biggar, within a few days of each other. From this front we moved south and on

Lt.-Col. G. R. Pearkes, V.C., D.S.O., M.C.

the 1st of April we were situated in the New Brunswick trench, in front of Méricourt.

During the last three months two important changes in our organization took place which it may be wise to record.

Major G. R. Pearkes, recently awarded the Victoria Cross for gallant work at Passchendaele with the 5th C.M.R., was appointed Officer Commanding 116th Battalion, to replace Colonel Sharpe, whose illness in England seemed likely to keep him away from France for an indefinite period.

Major J. Sutherland, at one time a Company Commander in the 52nd Battalion, but recently an instructor at Ferfay, was appointed second in command to Lt.-Colonel Pearkes.

The German grand offensive, which was to land him at the gates of Paris, had commenced, and in consequence the "staff" were showing very distinct signs of nervousness—commonly called "wind up."

The First, Second and Fourth Canadian Divisions had been, or were being withdrawn from the line to be in readiness for action wherever they might most be needed, and the Third Division was left to defend Vimy Ridge as best it could, with nothing behind it except its own artillery and a couple of labour battalions employed in agricultural work, which had lately become a feature of modern warfare. During the day the Brigadier paid a visit to Battalion Headquarters, and, amongst other things, suggested that we might carry out some kind of raid in order to get identification, and by this means discover the enemy plans.

At 6 p.m. a meeting of the Company Commanders was called, and within the hour it was arranged to send out a battle patrol of one officer and twenty-five O.R's. from each Company, to work independently on given frontages. It was also arranged that whichever patrol was successful in capturing a prisoner, would send up a red flare immediately. The operation was scheduled to commence at 11 p.m., without artillery or machine gun support.

At 9 p.m. a message was received from the Divisional Commander stating that identification on our front might be necessary, and at 10 p.m. the Corps Commander wired in saying that it *was* necessary, so that, all things considered, our preparations were probably well timed.

"D" Company patrol, under Captain Baird, was the first to start the quarry, for shortly after setting out it ran into a strong German patrol on its way over to our lines. With the battle cry "Come on Toronto," Captain Baird, followed by his patrol, rushed on the Germans before they had time to move and a regular scrimmage took place, during which Captain Baird lost the use of his right arm, due to the displacement of one of the muscles. He was in the act of capturing the German patrol leader when his right arm collapsed and his revolver dropped from his hand. The German officer immediately seized him round the neck

REST BILLETS 59

and was giving him a rough time when one of our party shot the German dead. In the meantime the remainder of our patrol had succeeded in capturing two prisoners and put the rest to flight.

Red flares were immediately sent up and all parties returned to our lines in high spirits, having obtained the "necessary identification" asked for by the Corps only two hours previously, although this achievement was greatly dimmed by the loss of two officers killed (Lt. J. A. Gibson and Lt. R. W. Soper).

It was during this tour that we received the following special order of the day from Field-Marshal Sir Douglas Haig:

To All Ranks of the British Army in France and Flanders:

"We are again at a crisis in the War. The enemy has collected on this front every available Division and is aiming at the destruction of the British Army. We have already inflicted on the enemy in the course of the last two days, very heavy loss, and the French are sending troops as quickly as possible to our support. I feel that everyone in the Army, fully realizing how much depends on the exertion and steadfastness of each one of us, will do his utmost to prevent the enemy from attaining his object."

And this did not add any particular comfort to our feelings.

The Germans, however, were not thinking just then

of retaking Vimy Ridge, but of pushing through to Paris along the line of least resistance, which, judging by the progress they were making, was around the front of the Fifth Army, the "Fighting Fifth," as they were afterwards called.

From the Méricourt front we were moved up north of Lens, and having put up with a lot of shelling and other annoyances from the Bosch, it was decided to take revenge by means of a stealth raid. "B" and "C" Companies each sent out a party consisting of one officer and twenty O.R's. "B" Company's party, under Lt. Dunlop, encountered the enemy in Nun's Alley Sap, where a tough fight took place before the Germans were finally overcome. Several of them threw up their hands as if to surrender and Lance-Corporal Hayward ran forward to secure these prisoners; instead of surrendering they seized Hayward, who had the greatest difficulty in extricating himself from their grip.

On the 30th of April the battalion moved away from the line, and with the other units of the Canadian Corps, became part of Foch's famous reserve, which was later to play such a prominent part in the final overthrow of the entire German Army. And so, during many days of glorious summer weather, and under the careful and expert guidance of Lt.-Col. G. R. Pearkes, V.C., the little old "Umpty Umps" made preparations for the future. It was during this period that we received the sad news of the death of Colonel Sam Sharpe in Montreal, on the 25th May.

SPECIAL ORDER OF THE DAY
By FIELD-MARSHAL SIR DOUGLAS HAIG
K.T., G.C.B., G.C.V.O., K.C.I.E
Commander-in-Chief, British Armies in France.

To ALL RANKS OF THE BRITISH ARMY IN FRANCE AND FLANDERS.

We are again at a crisis in the War. The enemy has collected on this front every available Division, and is aiming at the destruction of the British Army. We have already inflicted on the enemy in the course of the last two days very heavy loss, and the French are sending troops as quickly as possible to our support. I feel that everyone in the Army, fully realising how much depends on the exertions and steadfastness of each one of us, will do his utmost to prevent the enemy from attaining his object.

General Headquarters,
23rd March, 1918.

Commander-in-Chief,
British Armies in France.

PRINTED IN FRANCE BY ARMY PRINTING AND STATIONERY SERVICES. PRESS A—3/18.

One of the Original Orders received by the Battalion, during a Tour
in the Trenches opposite Mericourt

There is, perhaps, no more glorious monument to the memory of this gallant soldier than his letter written "in the Field" on October 21st, 1917, just before the battle of Passchendaele, in which he said: "If it should be my fate to be among those who fall, I wish to say I have no regrets to offer. I have done my duty as I saw it, and have fought in defence of those principles upon which our great Empire is founded, and I die without any fears as to the ultimate destiny of all that is immortal within me."

CHAPTER VIII.

August 8th.

ON the 6th July, after an unusually long rest from the line, the 116th Battalion relieved the P.P.C.L.I. in the Neuville Vitasse sector, situated about three miles south of Arras. The accommodation here was very poor, and considerable time was spent in building shelters.

Several important reconnaissances were made on this front, during which we lost Lt. S. D. Woodruff, killed; and 10 other ranks, wounded.

After spending 17 days in this area we were finally relieved by the 1st Canadian Infantry Battalion and moved back in reserve once more.

On the evening of August 5th, at Boves Wood, the battalion was resting in bivouacs, after a series of long night marches from rear areas, which were conducted with so much secrecy as to almost warrant the suggestion that we were being transferred to the Italian, or some other far distant front. Only recently a printed order entitled "Keep Your Mouth Shut," which dealt with the advisability of strict silence concerning all movements of troops or operations of a military nature, had been pasted in the pay book of every man in the Corps; so that whenever anyone on the line of march was over-curious about our destination there was always the simple answer, "Remember your pay book."

That we were still in France was evident, and that we were likely to remain there, if not permanently, at least for the next few weeks, was made known that evening at a Company Commanders' meeting, during which the C.O. announced the joyful news that the battalion would shortly be engaged in operations of a more comprehensive nature than night marching. There was evidently some method in our madness, and everyone was all attention, particularly since Company Commanders' meetings had lately been showing signs of monotony.

Very little was known, except that a battle of great importance was imminent, that Australian, British and French troops would likely be engaged, and that there would be scarcely any time for final preparations, which we had always been accustomed to in the past. The German grand offensive, which began in March, had only partially succeeded, although the battles of the Somme, Messines and Passchendaele had been neutralized by their recent gains.

The importance of carrying out, to the fullest extent, the training in open warfare which we had experienced during the summer, was particularly impressed.

The attack by our battalion was to be carried out on a frontage of one thousand yards, starting from the village of Hourges, and although a definite final objective was suggested, entailing an advance of some five thousand yards, there was nothing to prevent us from following through to twice or three times that distance, providing the circumstances proved favorable.

The general scheme for the battalion was as follows:— "A" Company (Capt. Ritchie) would attack on the right, going through to what was known as the Bade trench system, which they were to capture and consolidate. "C" Company (Capt. Sutton) would follow "A" Company, and working round the high ground on the left flank, would drive for the enemy defences north of Hammon Wood, thence push from the north edge of the Wood to the left of our final objective, and deal with certain enemy batteries presumed to be there. "D" Company (Capt. Baird) would follow "C" Company and, passing through "A" Company, would work around the northern slope of high ground and push for the eastern side of Hammon Wood. "B" Company (Capt. Preston) was to follow in reserve until the Bade system had been captured, when it would follow "D" Company and mop up Hammon Wood, "A" Company then coming into battalion reserve.

From a study of the map and intelligence provided it seemed that even with little opposition the turning movement to be made would be extremely difficult, and that the leaders of all units would be called upon to exercise their best judgment and skill in order to ensure success, especially in view of the fact that very little opportunity was to be given them for making a personal reconnaissance.

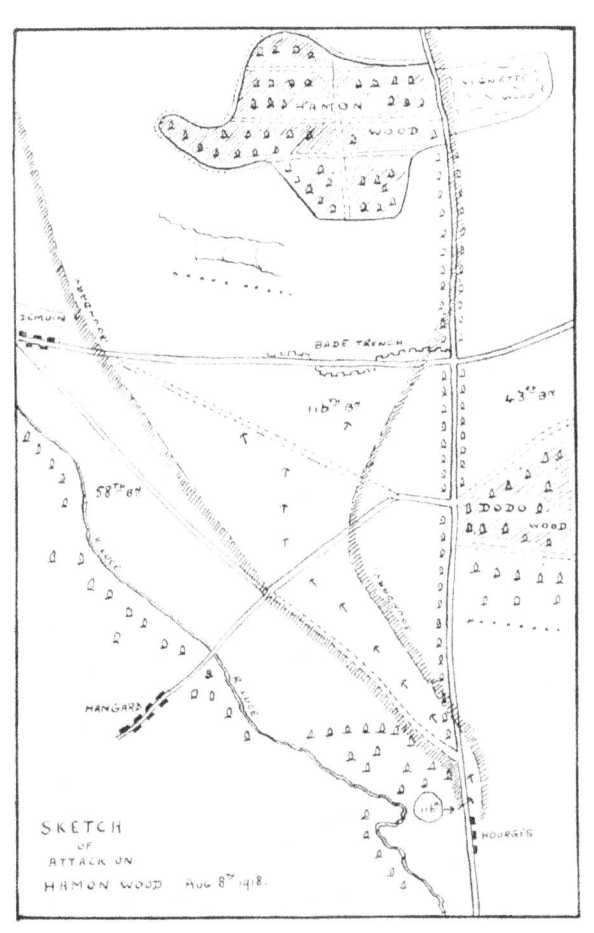

When it became generally known that the attack was imminent the spirits of the battalion ran high, and preparations for the great battle were pushed with all possible zeal.

The battalion moved from Boves to Gentelle Wood, a distance of six kilometres, moving out at 11 p.m., and arriving at 6 a.m. The congestion of traffic was the worst imaginable, and in consequence it was only with the greatest difficulty that any movement forward by infantry was possible, there being only one road of approach.

With but little sleep, reconnoitring commenced almost at once, and in order to observe secrecy, small parties were sent forward to Domart Wood. The Commanding Officer, Intelligence Officer and Company Commanders only were able to reach the forward system and make a quick reconnaissance at close range. Owing to the broken nature of the ground the assembly area was limited and positions for one company had to be found forward of the front line, held by the troops then holding that sector. All these areas were thoroughly reconnoitred and positions taped off, which was an extremely difficult and hazardous task due to the night activity of enemy machine guns, but thanks to the assistance of the Commander of the Australian Outpost Company then holding the line, who personally pointed out the most favorable positions, everything was completed satisfactorily.

At 9.30 p.m. on the night of August 7th the battalion

moved off to occupy the assembly positions. Zigzag lanes had been cut through the standing corn on both sides of the road and along one of these we moved in single file with as little noise as possible. Each man carried two water bottles, 48 hours' rations and 170 rounds of ammunition in addition to his usual battle equipment. To drown the curses of the weary troops as well as the approach of the tanks it had been arranged with great forethought, for a flight of heavy bombing planes to operate during the night in this area. It was a bright moonlight night, and the movement forward proceeded uninterrupted; the battalion scouts, acting as guides, led their platoons, and the slow task of crossing the river over bridge 53 commenced. Opened out to five paces interval, and trying to move quietly, made the march an exceptionally tedious one; however, the crossing was made successfully, and positions occupied under the personal supervision of those who had made the arrangements the night before.

It was by no means an easy position to attack from, as the leading company was facing south. The assembly was finally completed at 2.15 a.m., and word passed round that the zero hour would be at 4.20 a.m.; consequently there was still time to rest and to take up any minor details which might have been previously overlooked.

At 4.20 a.m. sharp, one of the greatest barrages in the history of the war by artillery and machine guns opened out. It was truly a marvellous piece of work considering no previous registration had been made.

The difficulty of getting away from the assembly points commenced at zero, plus eight minutes, and the greatest credit is due to the unit commanders for leading their companies and platoons out as well as they did. The left company were obliged to make a left-about wheel round a hedge, out to a road which they covered, and from there deploy in artillery formation. The remainder followed rapidly, and at zero plus forty minutes, the whole Battalion was clear of the jumping-off positions, including Headquarters, which followed in rear of the reserve company. The enemy retaliation came down quickly, but was not very heavy, although the congestion around the assembly point resulted in some casualties there.

The dense fog and smoke made it very difficult to preserve direction, and the Demuin road, with its tall trees, made an excellent landmark, previously noted, which enabled the 43rd, 58th and our own battalion to deploy towards their correct objectives. The enemy machine guns were then busy, and fighting commenced in earnest. "C" Company, on the left, realizing the necessity of pushing on as rapidly as possible, made excellent time. "A" Company got into the fight early, and suffered severe casualties, losing all their officers and about sixty other ranks before reaching their objective, and it was only through the prompt action of C. S. M. Fenwick, who gathered the remnants of that company together, that they were enabled to do so.

The tanks were very much handicapped by the

dense fog, and lost direction, operating on the flanks, with the exception of two, which nearly ran down a number of our battalion when they went through us at the start.

Very heavy fighting took place around enemy Headquarters. Machine guns were in abundance, and it was only after brilliant work on the part of the forward company that this nest was successfully dealt with, and a long stream of prisoners commenced leaving for the rear. The dash of our men was most marked, showing a marvellous difference from the old staid method of following the barrage shoulder to shoulder at the high port. Enemy machine gun nests were difficult to locate, owing to the poor observation, and a great many of these were cut off and surrendered to the infantry following behind.

Owing to a check which "A" Company received at the Hangard-Dodo Wood road, Battalion Headquarters soon found itself close to the battle and provided reinforcements to assist them in taking their final objective.

The advance had also been checked by machine gun fire immediately to the right centre and left of the Bade trench, and under cover of our own fire these nests were rushed and put out of action, severe casualties being inflicted on the enemy, their guns being captured and some prisoners taken.

An isolated field gun was still in action behind a small hedge approximately to the front and left of Bade trench; this was soon put out of action and the survivors of the crew captured. The advance was then continued and the Bade system finally taken with a number of machine guns, which were remounted on the parados ready for action by 6.15 a.m.; Battalion Headquarters was immediately established here, and the composite company ("A" Company, with Headquarter reinforcements) moved forward to provide a covering fire for "C" and "D" Companies in their advance on Hammon Wood.

Meanwhile, on the left, the advance was going along well, a great many machine guns being captured without interfering with the progress of our men. Close touch was kept on our left flank with the 58th Battalion, and owing to the extremely poor visibility, it was considered advisable to make certain that our left flank was secure at Demuin Wood before committing all our left flank platoons to the assault on Hammon Wood; consequently one platoon went into Demuin with the 58th Battalion.

It was not known exactly what progress the right was making at this time, and with depleted ranks, it seemed at the moment that the number of infantry available for the advance on Hammon Wood was none too strong. As the advance progressed the enemy were seen on the high ground 500 yards to the right, still in action and apparently firing on "A" Company in the Bade trench. Fire was immediately brought to bear on the rear of this party, and after a few rounds they were compelled to capitulate; again a large number of prisoners were sent to the rear. This enabled "B" Company to go up on the right and their appearance considerably heartened "C" Company, so that the advance against Hammon Wood pushed forward rapidly from west and north. It was also realized that "D" Company was making good progress, and were getting within reach of the Woods.

An enemy field-battery of two guns, still in action, was dealt with on the high ground to the north of Hammon Wood re-entrant, together with a number of machine guns.

Whilst "D" Company progressed forward on the right a composite company of "C" and "B" Companies pressed up the re-entrant from the north. The enemy artillery had evidently been reached before they had realized their danger; some of the gunners fought to a finish, firing through open sights on our men advancing until surrounded. A few rounds, together with the bold assault of infantry straight to the guns, was sufficient to prove to the enemy the futility of further resistance; consequently a record capture of enemy guns was made, and the survivors of the artillery group, who were numerous, came streaming from the dug-outs in which they had taken shelter, and were marched to the rear under their own officers. An eight-inch howitzer, a 5.9. and a 4.1 long-range battery were among the trophies captured, together with an artillery Quartermaster's stores, which contained all kinds of unknown material.

Along the high ground to the south and east some enemy machine guns still held out. These were quickly dealt with by "D" Company, and Hammon Wood was cleared. Our men now went well forward of the Wood and commenced firing on parties of the enemy infantry seen on a hill about a hundred yards to the left. A temporary defence system was rapidly established, and the ground cleared in front of the 7th Brigade, which was close behind and ready to push forward; and so by 7.30 a.m. our battalion had reached and consolidated its final objective, in which operations they captured 16 guns, 40 machine guns and about 450 prisoners.

Our casualties were 2 officers, Capt. A. W. Baird, M.C., Lt. J. Anderson, and 30 other ranks killed; 10 officers and 148 other ranks wounded and missing.

CHAPTER IX.

THE BOIRY SHOW.

SUCCESSFUL as our attack had been, we were not allowed to leave this area until after a further demonstration of our usefulness, and on the 11th instant we took over the line from remnants of the Royal Scots, Dorsets and Manchesters, who had run into stiff opposition in the neighborhood of Parvillers, and in consequence had suffered very heavy casualties. The situation was what is called obscure, and on the following day six of our platoons, in conjunction with the P.P.C.L.I. on the left, were rushed forward to capture Middle Wood and Square Wood. A number of machine guns fell into our hands, and identification was secured.

On the 13th the Germans counter-attacked and forced our outposts to retire slightly, and on the 16th we were relieved by the 19th Battalion and withdrew to Beaucourt Wood, having lost one officer, Lt. I. J. J. McCorkell, and thirteen other ranks killed; three officers, including Lt. A. H. Goodman, who died of wounds, and sixty-four other ranks wounded.

After a march by easy stages from the Amiens sector we finally reached "Y" huts on the 25th of August; old familiar rest homes of the Nissen variety on the Arras-St. Pol Road. The reports from all parts of the

GROUP TAKEN AT PERNES (DEC., 1918).

Back Row: Lt. E. B. Elliott; Lt. G. W. Morgan; Lt. C. R. Hillis (killed in action); Lt. A. L. MacDonald; Lt. H. K. Wood; Lt. F. A. MacGrotty (killed in action); Lt. W. E. Shier; Lt. G. E. Haygarth; Lt. W. A. Orr; Lt. J. B. Quarry; Lt. H. E. Patterson.
Third Row: Lt. R. W. Soper (killed in action); Lt. J. A. Hughes; Lt. J. A. Proctor (accidentally killed); Lt. W. J. Preston (killed in action); Lt. J. A. Gibson (killed in action); Lt. R. W. Biggar (killed in action); Lt. A. H. Dixon; Lt. J. A. Huggins; Lt. H. R. Williams; Lt. G. M. Leslie; Lt. T. A. Irwin; Lt. A. K. Wilson; Lt. T. H. Broad (killed in action).
Second Row: Capt. Armstrong, C.A.M.C.; Capt. D. Ritchie, O.C. A Coy.; Actg. Major E. P. S. Allen, O.C. (B Coy.); Major G. R. Pearkes, M.C. (2nd in Command); Lt.-Col. S. S. Sharpe, O.C. (accidentally killed); Capt. A. F. Hind (Adjutant); Capt. H. E. Ruwald, O.C. (C Coy); Capt. A. W. Baird, O.C. (D Coy) (killed in action); Capt. N. E. Fairhead (Quartermaster).
Front Row: Lt. W. A. Dunlop; Lt. L. V. Sutton; Lt. J. H. Hughes, M.C. (Transport Officer); Lt. K. L. Wallace; Lt. H. E. Gee.

THE BOIRY SHOW

line were most satisfactory, but we had not been allowed to while away the summer in training for nothing, and on the morning of the 26th we were again on the march in "battle order."

It was soon realized that something serious was on in front, our hearts being gladdened by the sight of six hundred or more Bosch prisoners, who were passed *en route* for the rear.

About midday, after marching through the picturesque old city of Arras, we halted on the outskirts of the city and made ourselves comfortable in cellars and ruined houses.

Along the line of march we had been busy among ourselves with conjectures as to what our next job was to be, and from information secured from walking wounded and others, we learned that the 8th Brigade C.M.R., after several days of fighting, had attacked and captured the village of Monchy Le Preu, a particularly fine piece of work, for Monchy was a hard nut to crack owing to its geographical situation on the high ground, situated about three miles east of Arras and just north of the Arras-Cambrai Road.

At 7 p.m. we moved forward again and at 11.30 p.m. reached and occupied shell holes just west of Monchy, very fortunately shown on the map as Orange Hill. On our arrival here orders were received from the 9th Brigade to co-operate with other units of the Brigade and attack at 4.55 a.m. A conference of Company Commanders was hastily called when the plan of attack was discussed and instructions quickly detailed, and at 12.10 midnight, companies had moved off by platoons to take up assembly positions in the jumping-off trench held by the Royal Canadian Regiment. It was a pitch dark night with no opportunity for looking over the ground, and very little time to explain to the men the objective and plan of attack. It was here that the results of summer training and night manoeuvres justified the many hours spent, all companies being in position by 4 a.m., thus giving all hands a breathing spell and an opportunity to explain details of the attack.

The Brigade objectives were Boiry-Notre-Dame, Artillery Hill, and the two woods known as Bois du Sart and Bois du Vert. The 58th Battalion objective was the Bois du Sart, and the 52nd Battalion the Bois du Vert. The 116th Battalion was to pass through these units and capture Boiry and Artillery Hill, the 43rd Battalion to follow in reserve. "A" Company (Capt. Preston) was to follow in close support to the 52nd Battalion, and on their clearing the wood was to follow through and make a turning movement north on Boiry Village. "D" Company (Capt. Wilson), followed by "C" Company (Capt. Sutton), were to work along the sunken road between the two woods and on their being cleared were to push on and capture Boiry and Artillery Hill, "B" Company (Major Pratt) to follow in close support of "C" and "D" Companies.

With an almost uncanny exactness our artillery barrage opened at 4.55 a.m., and being closely followed

THE BOIRY SHOW 75

by our front waves, the whole battalion was soon in the thick of the Bosch artillery and machine gun barrage.

After moving forward about a hundred yards our objectives were soon seen. The two woods situated on rising ground stood out in bold relief with the village of Boiry perched on the top of another and higher hill about 800 yards beyond the woods.

It was soon realized that the Bosch had a lot of kick left in him yet, "A" Company being forced to swing to the right of the Bois du Vert to clean up some machine gun nests which were inflicting heavy casualties on our forward platoons by enfilade fire. The enemy was in great strength here and it was not long before we were engaged in hand-to-hand fighting. During the day this line of trenches was captured, lost and recaptured by counter-attacks no less than three times.

During one of these attacks Sergt. McMillan of "A" Company was captured and forced by the Bosch to carry back wounded, but on his second trip he was recaptured in a counter-attack led by Capt. Preston.

In the meantime the 58th and 52nd Battalions, after hard fighting, had captured their objectives and "D" and "C" Companies of our own Battalion had cleaned up the ground between the woods, but on emerging to the open ground in advance of these they were literally mown down by intense machine gun fire from Artillery Hill and Boiry Village. It was here, whilst gallantly trying to lead forward the advance, that Major J. Sutherland, acting in command of the battalion, was killed, the command then falling on Major Pratt, next senior officer.

Owing to the intense machine gun fire it was found impossible to make any great advance without further support, but during the day individual and small parties made further gains and a line was finally established well in advance of the woods, communication being established with the 58th and 52nd Battalions on our left and right.

On night falling every effort was made to reorganize the companies and platoons. The evacuation of th wounded was rendered most difficult, as were the ration and ammunition carrying parties, owing to the continuous machine gun fire and the fact that we were occupying shell holes with very little cover. During the night, orders were received to make a further attack in conjunction with other units of the 9th Brigade on Artillery Hill from the Bois du Sart; on the morning of the 28th Aug., after getting into our assembly positions this order was cancelled, and we were ordered to take up new ground and closely support the 4th C.M.R. Battalion in a flank movement from the south of the Bois du Vert, in conjunction with other units of the 3rd Division.

At 11 a.m., "zero hour," our artillery laid down a perfect barrage and both Boiry and Artillery Hill were captured with a large number of prisoners, a line being established just on the outskirts of the town. At 9.30 p.m. very welcome orders were received that our division

THE BOIRY SHOW 77

would be relieved by the 4th British Division and at 3.10 a.m. on the 29th of August the 116th Battalion was relieved by a battalion of the Hampshire Regiment, companies moving off independently when relieved and assembling in billets in Feuchy.

In these two days of fighting our losses were three officers, Major J. Sutherland, D.S.O., Lt. H. D. Livingstone, Lt. R. Campkin, and forty-two other ranks killed, seven officers and two hundred and forty-three other ranks wounded or missing.

On the 17th September the battalion was resting in the Guemappe area, close to the scene of the fighting described above, and about 5 p.m. the German artillery suddenly commenced to register on our camp with 5.9's; several men standing round the field kitchens were killed, and a number wounded. One of these shells burst within a few yards of a party of our officers who were on their way over to look after casualties, and Captain F. W. Ott and Captain T. H. Broad, both of whom came over to France with the battalion, were killed. Colonel Pearkes and Lt. Proctor were wounded, the former very seriously. This was a terrible blow to the battalion, coming on top of the very severe casualties we had experienced during the last month, and left us incidentally *sans* Colonel, second in command (Major Sutherland); Adjutant (Captain Ott); Intelligence Officer (Captain Broad); and Scout Officer (Lt. Proctor). The general surroundings and our recent losses had a most depressing effect on the whole battalion, and we were glad when orders were received to move back to Arras, which was accomplished on the 19th, under the command of Major Pratt.

Later we were moved back a few more miles to "Y" huts, already mentioned, and which was just across the road from the Casualty Clearing Station in which Colonel Pearkes was lying dangerously ill.

Arriving in France with the 8th Canadian Infantry Brigade in 1915, Private G. R. Pearkes proceeded to win a commission in the field, and as a Lieutenant in the same brigade was awarded the Military Cross for gallant conduct during the Somme offensive of 1916—although he had been wounded three times he continued in his upward career, and as a Company Commander in the 5th C.M.R., with the acting rank of Major, he won the Victoria Cross for conspicuous gallantry during the Battle of Passchendaele. It was then that the Divisional Commander (General Lipsett) selected him out of all other officers in the 3rd Division to fill the vacancy of 2nd in Command to the 116th Battalion.

All the previous honors won by him together with his almost unequalled experience were immediately centred in the welfare of our unit, and undoubtedly the high state of fighting efficiency and organization attained by us was greatly due to his unerring judgment and unselfish devotion to the battalion.

As our Commanding Officer in the battle of Amiens he was awarded the D.S.O. and French Croix de Guerre, and although not permitted to lead the battalion against

Boiry his influence and support behind were strongly felt by all ranks throughout this action and assisted us greatly in gaining our objectives. Wounded severely for the fifth time, it seemed hopeless to expect that he could survive. To the surprise and joy of everyone he rejoined us later at the Armistice Line in time to lead the triumphant march through Belgium and to return with us to Canada.

CHAPTER X.

CAMBRAI.

ON the evening of the 26th September we were off again in the direction of Cambrai, and after a cold and tedious train journey we arrived at Quéant about 1.30 a.m. on the 27th. The guides, who had been sent on in advance, seemed to have got lost, for they did not meet us at Quéant Station, and a certain amount of confusion ensued in consequence, before it was decided in which direction was situated a certain map location given us by Brigade Headquarters as our billeting area.

The rain poured down in buckets, and everyone was drenched to the skin by the time we reached our destination; however, the cooks got busy and a hot meal was served, soon after which we received orders to move forward. It should be mentioned here that Major D. Carmichael, D.S.O., M.C., second in command of the 58th Battalion, and one of the outstanding officers of the 9th Brigade, was transferred to us as Officer Commanding just after leaving "Y" huts.

The roads were packed with transport and guns coming up from every direction, and we picked our way by overland routes to Inchy, and from there to our new area, east of the Canal du Nord.

The kitchens were unable to move with us, and we

CAMBRAI 81

bivouacked in shell holes that night with no covering except waterproof sheets, and no hot dinner. About 3 a.m. the next morning the kitchens arrived, and the men gathered round them in small groups to try and get warm. It is surprising how good a thick bacon sandwich is with a ration of rum, about 5 o'clock in the morning!

About 7 a.m. the battalion moved forward, according to plan, closely following the 58th Battalion, through Bourlon Wood, which had been captured only a few hours previously by the 4th Division, and by 10 a.m. we were assembled behind a railway embankment to the east of Bourlon, and in full view of the city of Cambrai. Up to this time we had encountered nothing more than scattered shell fire, and we had had no casualties.

From our embankment we watched some tanks coming out of action, and at 6.30 p.m. we received verbal instructions that the 58th Battalion would attack the Marcoing Line, and that the 116th Battalion, passing through the 58th, would attack and capture the Village of St. Olle, which is a small suburb of Cambrai.

Zero hour was set for 7 p.m., and in consequence there was no time to discuss any plan of operation beyond the fact that "A" Company (Capt. Preston) and "B" Company (Capt. Orr) would lead the attack. By the time we had reached our positions it was dark.

The attack by the 58th was successful, and we moved through their lines in the direction of St. Olle. Judging by the machine gun fire the village was strongly held, and as no reconnaissance of the ground could be made, and only a very general direction maintained, it was decided that we would not proceed with the attack until daylight.. Battalion Headquarters was established, and rations were brought forward and distributed to the companies under the very nose of the Bosch, who could have wiped us out if he had only known; and so darkness has sometimes its advantages also. During the night it was possible to make some preparation, and at 6 a.m. the next morning "A" and "B" Companies, with "C" Company (Capt. Williams) and "D" Company (Capt. Patterson) in support, resumed the attack.

The leading platoons had scarcely started when they were caught between cross belts of machine gun fire, coming from a small trench in front of St. Olle and Petit Fontaine on the right, and after an hour's fighting they had hardly made any headway at all, and had lost practically the whole of their effectives. News of this disaster was brought by Lieutenant Smith of "B" Company, who rolled over the parapet of the trench just outside Battalion Headquarters in an exhausted condition. From all he said, it appeared that "A" and "B" Companies had been annihilated; that Captain Preston and Lieutenant Palmer were both wounded and prisoners, and that Lieutenant Norton had been killed. This information was corroborated by Private Stankewicz, who had been taken prisoner with Captain Preston, but who later escaped to our lines.

Under these distressing conditions it seemed almost

GROUP OF OFFICERS AT BLANDAIN, 1919. (Canadian Official Copyright)

Back Row.—Lt. A. B. Bonner, M.M., D.S.O.; Lt. L. W. Barton, M.C.; Lt. W. R. Barton; Lt. J. R. Leslie; Capt. L. V. Sutton, M.C.
Third Row.—Lt. G. W. Morgan; Lt. G. E. Wallis; Capt. J. A. Hughes, M.C.; Lt. T. A. Smith, M.C.
Lt. W. H. Montague, Padre; Capt. Goselle; Lt. A. S. Peeke; Lt. F. T. H. Youngman, M.C.; Capt. A. M. Closse; Lt.
D. M. Waterous; Capt. E. C. Harris (C.A.M.C.); Capt. H. E. Patterson, M.C.; Lt. M. Crabtree, M.C.; Lt. E. J. Sager; Lt.
H. J. A. Painter.
Second Row.—Capt. J. H. Hughes, M.C. (Quartermaster); Capt. A. K. Wilson, M.C., O.C. "A" Coy.; Capt. E. P. S. Allen, D.S.O.
(Adjutant); Major A. W. Pratt, D.S.O. (2nd in Command); Lt. Col. C. R. Peakes, V.C., D.S.O., M.C. (O.C.); Major A. F. Hind
D.C. (D Coy); Capt. W. A. Dunlop, M.C., O.C. B Coy.; Capt. R. H. Moody, O.C. C Coy.; Capt. C. M. Sheppard
Front Row.—Lt. R. R. Hocsis (Transport Off'r); Lt. E. Pearson; Lt. J. A. Triffin; Lt. T. M. Wylie

as if our gallant unit would fail, for the first time, to win its objective. A battery of our Field Artillery were in action about one thousand yards directly to our rear and a messenger was despatched at once to explain the situation to the Battery Commander, and, if possible, obtain his assistance.

Fire was immediately brought to bear on the machine gun positions in the St. Olle trench, and the work by this battery, in conjunction with our own Lewis guns, was so effective that it was possible to work two platoons from "C" and "D" Companies around the north-west of the village, and Lt. Bonner, who was placed in command of the operation, succeeded with consummate skill and bravery, in rushing the St. Olle trench, destroying a large number of the enemy and capturing one hundred prisoners with ten heavy machine guns.

"D" Company was then able to push through the village as far as the junction of the Arras-Cambrai and Bapaume-Cambrai roads, along which posts were immediately established, and the remnants of "A" and "B" Companies were withdrawn to Battalion Headquarters.

If Fritz had not been so concerned about his own safety at this time he might have found the retaking of St. Olle a very easy matter, for after practically three days and nights without sleep the resisting powers of the gallant "Umpty Umps" were fast waning.

On account of the severe casualties the battalion was reduced to three companies, each one having an average strength of ninety rifles, and orders were issued by the Brigadier to make use of the Battalion Band and Bugles, as the attack was to be continued on the first of October.

Such things had happened to other units we knew, but we certainly did not relish the thought of losing our "music," although the "music" itself, with the true battalion spirit, was game to the core. During the day Major Carmichael, with Major Pratt and Lieutenant Bonner, made a reconnaissance of the ground immediately between us and Cambrai, and were very nearly put out of business by our own heavy artillery, which had started to register without warning, on the junction of the Arras-Cambrai and Bapaume-Cambrai roads.

All that night it poured with rain, but towards dawn the weather commenced to clear, and companies moved off from their positions around St. Olle, "D" Company leading, followed by "C", "B" and Headquarters. An intense artillery barrage was encountered whilst crossing the Douai-Cambrai Road, and the battalion suffered quite a number of casualties. Major Carmichael was badly wounded in the face, and gave instructions to Captain Allen, the next senior officer, to take over the remnants of the battalion.

On our left we could see the 4th Division advancing in artillery formation, lines of men in single file going steadily forward as if nothing could stop them; it was most inspiring, and everyone started cheering.

It seemed somehow that the Germans were at last

CAMBRAI 85

beaten, and that the war would soon be over, but our feelings of jubilation were a little previous, for after progressing about a mile our leading companies were stopped by a withering fire coming from the right flank.

On observation we discovered a battery of field guns, and quickly changing front, we engaged them with Lewis gun and rifle fire. By this means we managed to work up within close range, and most of the crews being killed or wounded the remainder disappeared over the brow of the hill. Following up closely it was found that they had taken up a position in a small triangular wood, which we eventually surrounded and captured, together with about eighty prisoners, four machine guns, and the battery of field guns mentioned above.

"D" Company and some sections of "C" Company then advanced slightly, taking up positions in front of the wood and facing Ramillies. Whilst holding this line they came under very heavy fire, and a battery of "whizz-bangs" opened on them at point blank range. For an hour or two the situation was most uncomfortable. The battalion on our right had been held up, and the 4th Division on our left had been forced to retire, leaving both our flanks in the air.

Reorganization in our present precarious position was out of the question, and after hanging on for two hours we decided to withdraw behind the western slope of the hill, where we established ourselves in a line of rifle pits, and got in touch with our right and left flanks. By this time the men were thoroughly exhausted, and news was gladly received that the 24th Battalion would relieve us that evening.

Our total casualties for the last four days' fighting around Cambrai were four hundred all ranks killed, wounded and missing.

CHAPTER XI.

Mons.

THROUGHOUT the whole operation around Cambrai the officers, N.C.O's. and men showed a wonderful devotion to duty, and an indomitable spirit to push forward. The difficulty of taking a well-organized system of enemy defences was considerably increased owing to the fact that there had been no opportunity for anyone to reconnoitre the assembly positions, or view the grounds over which we attacked, also the time which could be devoted to explaining to the men even the smallest outline of the plan of attack was almost negligible.

The greatest features were the taking of St. Olle after two of our companies had been practically wiped out; and the crossing of the Douai-Cambrai Road under a barrage of German heavy artillery. The good work by our battalion was recognized by the Divisional Commander who mentioned us in his special order of the day concerning these battles—in his own words:

"I wish to express my appreciation of the work done by the different Units of the Division, and by the Formations co-operating with us, during the past four days' fighting.

"The 7th Canadian Infantry Brigade under Brig.-General J. A. Clarke, D.S.O., and the 9th Canadian Infantry Brigade under Brig.-Gen. D. M. Ormond, D.S.O., have maintained their organization through difficult and sustained fighting.

"*The work of the 116th Canadian Infantry Battalion has been especially fine, etc., etc.*
"(Signed) F. O. W. LOOMIS,
(Major-General)
"2-10-'18 Commanding 3rd Canadian Div."

As soon as the relief had been completed by the 24th Battalion we were moved back behind Cambrai and camped in a sunken road just in front of Bourlon Wood. From here we retired by easy stages to Quéant, which we reached on the 10th of October, and having been allotted a section of the old Hindenburg trench, we started in to make ourselves at home and to nurse our wounds.

It was during our stay here that H.R.H. the Prince of Wales paid us an informal visit. At the time of his arrival the companies were scattered around the area, carrying out some Lewis gun training, and the Adjutant was in his shirt sleeves, making some improvements to his trench shelter.

Major Younger, the Brigade Major, rushed up to the Adjutant and asked for the C.O. (Major Pratt). "I'm sure I don't know where he is," said the Adjutant. "Oh, well," said the B.M., "you'll do. The Prince of Wales is just outside, and wants to go round and see the companies, so hurry up and get some clothes on and come and be presented." (Scene of great excitement,

N.C.O.'s at Brandon, 1916. (Canadian Official Copyright)

MONS 89

during which hats, coats, and belts were nowhere to be found, and finally the young Prince, highly amused, is conducted round by the hatless and much embarrassed adjutant.)

Later, Major Pratt was found, and introduced to our distinguished visitor, but not catching his name, stepped forward, and seizing his hand, said, "Pleased to meet you, I'm sure." But the Prince of Wales is a prince of good fellows, and despite the seeming want of courtesy shown him, pronounced himself highly pleased with his visit.

In the afternoon, all the officers of the battalion, together with a composite company of one hundred other ranks, attended the funeral of Major-General Lipsett, who was killed by a sniper whilst reconnoitring the forward positions. During his command of the 3rd Canadian Division (he had only recently been transferred to the Imperial Forces) his keen interest in the welfare of all ranks under his command had made him one of the most popular officers in the Canadian Corps.

On the 17th of the month, the 9th Brigade was inspected by the Corps Commander in a large and muddy field just north of Quéant. The Corps Commander, as most of the Corps know, was by no means a small man, and amongst the troops inspected were a number of men who had recently joined us, and who had consequently no idea as to whom the inspecting officer might be—also the ration of bread at that time was one loaf to three men. It was towards the end of the inspection, and the small squad of brass caps was walking down the ranks of a certain platoon—one of the newcomers took one look at the Corps Commander and remarked in a loud undertone, "Gee Whiz! Fancy being three men on a loaf with that old beggar."

The German Army was now in full retreat, and from intelligence received, it seemed likely that from now on we would have a difficult task in even keeping in touch with it. Starting on the 22nd of the month we began a series of advances, which only ended when the Armistice terms had been signed and the Armistice line established about five miles east of Mons.

This advance through country and villages, which had so long been occupied by a cruel and overbearing enemy, will live forever in the memories of all who took part in it. The people seemed to be crazed with the joy of liberty—there wasn't anything they wouldn't do for "les braves Canadiens," as they called us—flowers were strewn along the streets, bouquets were showered on us, and even kisses. Wine was dug up from where it had been hastily cached in 1914, and from personal experience we can assert that it showed no sign of deterioration for its four years' rest.

These were good days for France, and for us, too, and on the 10th of November we were billeted in a small town called Wasmuel, waiting for orders to take over the front line, at present occupied by the 7th Brigade. At about 8 o'clock on the morning of the 11th November the following order arrived from Brigade H.Q.:

"The 116th Battalion will move up forthwith and take over the line from the 7th Brigade, holding a front line from Q. 9 central to K. 19 central aaa. After taking over the line the battalion will stand fast aaa. *Hostilities will cease at 11 a.m. to-day aaa.* All precautions to be taken against the enemy aaa. No intercourse with the enemy whatever to take place aaa. O.C. 116th Battalion will report to 9th Brigade H.Q. immediately, and will receive instructions as to route. Acknowledge."

It didn't take long to acknowledge such news as that, nor was there any delay in finding a runner to carry the tidings round to the companies, and by 9 a.m. the battalion was moving forward in the direction of Mons, over practically the same ground that our "contemptible little army" had made its gallant stand in August, 1914. The relief completed, a party of one hundred men from the rear details, including the brass band, represented the Battalion at a demonstration held in the public square in Mons, to celebrate the liberation of the City, and in the meantime we advanced our line somewhat, taking up positions along the Brussels-Mons Road, with Headquarters in Nimy.

At 5.30 the following morning the whole neighborhood was awakened by a series of explosions, which bore a striking resemblance to the fire from field artillery; for about half an hour we had an uncomfortable feeling that the war had started again, but on investigation discovered an enemy ammunition train, which had been set on fire by some very small and truly patriotic young Belgians.

THE 116TH BATTALION IN FRANCE

Later in the day our line was still further advanced, and we finally occupied what was to be known as the Armistice Line, and from which no advance could be made until the expiration of a definite time limit.

Our left flank, which rested on the Brussels-Mons Road, proved to be a source of great trouble and annoyance, since we received explicit orders to allow no one to pass either from east to west or west to east, except those carrying a special permit signed by 3rd Canadian Divisional H.Q.

Our posts along this road were harassed daily by a continuous barrage of civilians, wishing to pass through from both sides, and naturally peeved at being refused permission. In addition the number of staff officers and generals who clamored to proceed to Brussels, was almost unlimited. The "Umpty Umps" had never seen so many red caps in the front line before; in fact, we scarcely knew that there were so many of them in the whole of the British Army.

"What do you mean by stopping my car?" said one rather fat and irate general. "I'm General 'so-and-so of the so-and-so's'." "I'm sorry, sir, but my instructions are absolutely definite, and unless you have a pass, etc., etc."—and back he had to go to Mons and get it.

And here ended the active service of our gallant unit, for when the first and second Canadian Divisions started their advance to the Rhine our posts were withdrawn, and on December 26th, after marching as far as Brussels with the object of relieving the First Division in Germany,

Battalion Colours Arrival at Exhibition Grounds, Toronto (1919)

MONS 93

we suddenly received orders to "about turn." We accomplished this in two beats of quick time instead of the usual three, and marched to Blandain, on the borders of France and Belgium, from which place, passing through Le Havre, we were transported to Bramshott via Weymouth, England, and thence to Canada.

"It's a long, long way to Tipperary,
But my heart's right there."

Honor Roll, showing the names of all ranks of the 116th Battalion who were killed in action or died of wounds or sickness, whilst on the service roll of the Battalion in France, between February, 1917, and February, 1919. This roll was compiled from the Service records of the Battalion, and is complete so far as the records will allow.

It is very much regretted that the names of those men who died of wounds or sickness, after having been evacuated to England or Canada do not all appear in this roll, owing to the fact that no official record was sent to the Battalion of such cases.

Lt. J. Anderson
(Killed in action)

Capt. A. W. Baird, M.C. & Bar
(Killed in action)

Lt. R. W. Biggar
(Killed in action)

Capt. T. H. Broad
(Killed in action)

Lt. R. Campkin
(Died of wounds)

Lt. C. V. V. Coombs
(Died Dec. 26th, 1919)

Lt. J. J. Doble
(Killed in action)

Lt. W. K. Kift
(Died of wounds)

Lt. J. A. Gibson
(Died of wounds)

Lt. A. H. Goodman
(Died of wounds)

Lt. C. R. Hillis
(Died of wounds)

Lt. T. W. Hutchison
(Died of wounds)

Lt. C. S. Lennox
(Died of wounds)

Lt. V. C. Lick
(Killed in action)

Lt. H. D. Livingston
(Killed in action)

Lt. F. A. MacGrotty
(Killed in action)

Lt. H. L. Major
(Died of wounds)

Lt. I. J. J. McCorkell
(Killed in action)

Lt. F. S. Neil
(Killed in action)

Lt. C. A. Norton
(Killed in action)

Capt. F. W. Ott, M.C.
(Killed in action)

Capt. W. J. Preston, M.C. & Bar
(Died of wounds)

Lt. J. A. Proctor
(Accidentally killed)

Lt. G. W. Robinson
(Died Nov. 11th, 1918)

Major J. Sutherland, D.S.O.
(Killed in action)

Lt. R. W. Soper
(Killed in action)

Lt. G. R. Weber
(Killed in action)

Lt. S. D. Woodruff
(Killed in action)

HONOR ROLL 95

Regt. No.	Rank	Name	Address
	Lt.-Col.	Sharpe, S. S. (D.S.O.)...	Uxbridge, Ont.
	Major	Sutherland, J. (D.S.O.)	Winnipeg, Man.
	Capt.	Baird, A. W. (M.C.)......	Toronto, Ont.
	Capt.	Broad, T. H...............	Calgary, Alta.
	Capt.	Ott, F. W. (M.C.)..........	Port Credit, Ont.
	Capt.	Preston, W. J. (M.C.)...	Toronto, Ont.
	Lieut.	Anderson, J...............	Sault Ste. Marie, Ont.
	Lieut.	Biggar, R. W...............	Hamilton, Ont.
	Lieut.	Campkin, R...............	Brampton, Ont.
	Lieut.	Coombs, C. V. V..........	Toronto, Ont.
	Lieut.	Doble, J. J.................	Sunderland, Ont.
	Lieut.	Gibson, J. A...............	Woodstock, Ont.
	Lieut.	Goodman, A. H...........	Toronto, Ont.
	Lieut.	Hillis, C. R.................	Hamilton, Ont.
	Lieut.	Hutchison, T. W...........	Uxbridge, Ont.
	Lieut.	Kift, W. K..................	Cannington, Ont.
	Lieut.	Lennox, C. S...............	Toronto, Ont.
	Lieut.	Lick, V. C..................	Beachville, Ont.
	Lieut.	Livingston, H. D...........	Brantford, Ont.
	Lieut.	MacGrotty, F. A...........	Whitby, Ont.
	Lieut.	Major, H. L................	Whitevale, Ont.
	Lieut.	McCorkell, I. J. J..........	Beaverton, Ont.
	Lieut.	Neil, F. S...................	Harriston, Ont.
	Lieut.	Norton, C. A...............	Midland, Ont.
	Lieut.	Proctor, J. A...............	Beaverton, Ont.
	Lieut.	Robinson, G. W...........	Toronto, Ont.
	Lieut.	Soper, R. W................	Uxbridge, Ont.
	Lieut.	Weber, G. R................	Hamilton, Ont.
	Lieut.	Woodruff, S. D.............	St. Catharines, Ont.

THE 116TH BATTALION IN FRANCE

Regt. No.	Rank	Name	Address
679272	C.S.M.	MacMillan, A. C. (M.M.)	Toronto, Ont.
643810	CQMS.	Penman, A.	Orillia, Ont.
644559	Sgt.	Braden, N. J. (M.M.)	Sebright, Ont.
746277	Sgt.	Brooks, R. F.	Toronto, Ont.
678241	Sgt.	Caulfield, S. J.	Toronto, Ont.
746278	Sgt.	Chapman, A. E.	Bilton, York, Eng.
775472	Sgt.	Dennison, S. O.	Inglewood, Ont.
745308	Sgt.	Drew, O. C.	Cannington, Ont.
745825	Sgt.	Fuller, C. O.	Watford, Ont.
775495	Sgt.	Hostrawser, G.	Malton, Ont.
776085	Sgt.	Howson, R. C.	Wingham, Ont.
679270	Sgt.	Keller, H. A.	Toronto, Ont.
678508	Sgt.	Knibbs, A. M.	Toronto, Ont.
644615	Sgt.	Picotte, N. E.	Penetang, Ont.
757875	Sgt.	Randle, A. E.	Hamilton, Ont.
690761	Sgt.	Stout, R. J.	Hamilton, Ont.
228441	Sgt.	Waldrum, D. D. K.	Toronto, Ont.
643985	Sgt.	Wheatley, J. A.	Elmvale, Ont.
745607	L.-Sgt.	Blunden, W. J.	Madeley, Salop, Eng.
679254	L.-Sgt.	Fell, W. G. A.	Toronto, Ont.
644405	Cpl.	Arnold, P. A.	Midland, Ont.
678537	Cpl.	Brittan, L. F. (M.M.)	Hamilton, Ont.
678545	Cpl.	Butchers, A.	Plymouth, Eng.
745250	Cpl.	Campbell, J.	Woodville, Ont.
775262	Cpl.	Crawford, R.	Detroit, Mich.
681305	Cpl.	Daniells, F. B.	Toronto, Ont.
690461	Cpl.	Doan, J. E. (M.M.)	Hamilton, Ont.
802019	Cpl.	Doughty, E. R.	London, Ont.
745085	Cpl.	Hawkins, W. H. K.	Guelph, Ont.

HONOR ROLL 97

Regt. No.	Rank	Name	Address
643807	Cpl.	Hinchcliffe, L...............	Orillia, Ont.
868008	Cpl.	Hood, G. W...............	Port Perry, Ont.
644408	Cpl.	Irwin, R. C...............	Midland, Ont.
228307	Cpl.	Lawrence, J. H............	Toronto, Ont.
775520	Cpl.	Maltby, A. E...............	Thornton Heath, Eng.
228302	Cpl.	McConnell, H. G..........	Toronto, Ont.
644083	Cpl.	McLean, H.................	Orillia, Ont.
678087	Cpl.	Orange, E..................	Nottingham, Eng.
678664	Cpl.	Rivers, T. L...............	Toronto, Ont.
868015	Cpl.	Shannon, E. G.............	Islington, Ont.
678438	Cpl.	Turner, P. (D.C.M.)......	Shelburne, Ont.
745931	L.-C.	Branch, B. W..............	Bowmanville, Ont.
745946	L.-C.	Coulter, W. H.............	Oshawa, Ont.
2507310	L.-C.	Deane, T. J...............	Liverpool, Eng.
868303	L.-C.	Elliott, H. L...............	Elizabethville, Ont.
775501	L.-C.	Howe, S....................	Cromarty, Ont.
644025	L.-C.	McKerrall, C..............	Coldwater, Ont.
678643	L.-C.	McKinnell, G..............	Cheshire, Eng.
644073	L.-C.	Middleton, W.R.(DCM)	Coldwater, Ont.
757380	L.-C.	Millar, C...................	Hamilton, Ont.
643999	L.-C.	Newlove, W. M............	Bradford, Yorks, Eng.
644611	L.-C.	Peacock, J. L..............	Penetanguishene, Ont.
644838	L.-C.	Reynolds, D. J.............	Anten Mills, Ont.
802004	L.-C.	Ross, I. D. (M.M.)........	Newmarket, Ont.
678922	L.-C.	Smith, G...................	Toronto, Ont.
678218	L.-C.	Spiroff, J..................	Toronto, Ont.
1004145	Pte.	Aaron, W...................	Oshwegan, Ont.
838469	Pte.	Adair, C. R.................	Mount Forest, Ont.
757925	Pte.	Adams, L. R................	Caistorville, Ont.

98   THE 116TH BATTALION IN FRANCE

Regt. No.	Rank	Name	Address
3025008	Pte.	Allan, Wm...................	Markinch, Scotland.
678759	Pte.	Allen, A. J	Much Wenlock, Eng.
3106609	Pte.	Allen, W. R...................	Sunderland, Eng.
663303	Pte.	Anderson, A. E.............	Acton West, Ont.
2562384	Pte.	Andison, R...................	Edinburgh, Scotland
2537460	Pte.	Arnold, R.....................	Leicester, Eng.
270639	Pte.	Armstrong, T...............	Dunnville, Ont.
644413	Pte.	Archer, A. V.................	Waverly, Ont.
104111	Pte.	Arnold, O. S.................	Hanwell, Middx., Eng.
757835	Pte.	Ashbough, A................	Hamilton, Ont.
249195	Pte.	Atkins, J.......................	Toronto, Ont.
249793	Pte.	Atkinson, W. G............	Co. Down, Ireland
690265	Pte.	Barlow, C.....................	Paris, Ont.
851074	Pte.	Bain, R.........................	Plymouth, Mass.
745768	Pte.	Bailey, A.......................	Toronto, Ont.
691013	Pte.	Bale, W. H...................	Darwen, Lancs., Eng.
3030462	Pte.	Barker, A......................	Frankford, U.S.A.
2507382	Pte.	Barnes, J. A..................	Boston, U.S.A.
542535	Pte.	Bewley, S. C.................	Toronto, Ont.
2255301	Pte.	Beckett, T. J.................	Cardinal, Ont.
643847	Pte.	Bentley, F.....................	Orillia, Ont.
679023	Pte.	Bennett, C....................	Torrington, Eng.
644564	Pte.	Beauchamp, I...............	Penetanguishene, Ont.
3030410	Pte.	Bencraft, W. L..............	Arlington, N.Y.
663532	Pte.	Berry, G. G...................	Lisle, Ont.
3030163	Pte.	Beddows, E. A..............	Liverpool, England
868262	Pte.	Bellbody, W. J..............	Uxbridge, Ont.
2591293	Pte.	Beveridge, J. J..............	Dunfermline, Scotland
678525	Pte.	Binkley, N....................	Hanover, Ont.

HONOR ROLL

Regt. No.	Rank	Name	Address
868257	Pte.	Blatchford, E. A.	Brownsville, Ont.
663235	Pte.	Blair, J.	Georgetown, Ont.
679031	Pte.	Boyce, R.	Toronto, Ont.
264420	Pte.	Borden, V. L.	Detroit, Mich.
643839	Pte.	Borman, George	Orillia, Ont.
757258	Pte.	Bowerbank, E. A.	Hamilton, Ont.
1063070	Pte.	Bolton, F.	Burleigh Falls, Ont.
2537404	Pte.	Bowerbank, T. W.	Tuxedo Park, N.Y.
249537	Pte.	Boucher, P. L.	Masson, Que.
757263	Pte.	Bowerbank, J. T.	Hamilton, Ont.
868201	Pte.	Brown, W. A.	London, England
690569	Pte.	Brownlie, A.	Hamilton, Ont.
757725	Pte.	Brain, T. W.	Hamilton, Ont.
644560	Pte.	Braithwaite, W. H.	Lefaives Corners, Ont.
264384	Pte.	Brewster, E.	Boaz, Ala.
850478	Pte.	Brown, A. C.	Shallow Lake, Ont.
690207	Pte.	Bremner, R. R.	Hamilton, Ont.
3105671	Pte.	Briggs, T.	Fall River, Mass.
863115	Pte.	Brown, B. J.	Toronto, Ont.
2304464	Pte.	Brophy, J. Dennis	Burlington, Vermont
1027596	Pte.	Burchfield, R. L.	Ithaca, N.Y.
3310041	Pte.	Burke, H. A.	Canfield, Ont.
3105833	Pte.	Burns, J.	Montreal, Que.
853399	Pte.	Campbell, W. A.	Vasey, Ont.
745250	Pte.	Campbell, J.	Woodville, Ont.
775458	Pte.	Campkin, S.	Brampton, Ont.
868316	Pte.	Campbell, John H.	Hillier, Ont.
2537328	Pte.	Callow, A. W.	Toronto, Ont.
121593	Pte.	Carroll, J.	England

THE 116TH BATTALION IN FRANCE

Regt. No.	Rank	Name	Address
644437	Pte.	Church, F. J.	Midland, Ont.
3106344	Pte.	Church, O.	Woodstock, Ont.
690466	Pte.	Churches, D. S.	Hamilton, Ont.
679317	Pte.	Christo, E.	Macedonia, Greece
3106697	Pte.	Ciuciulette, J.	Roumania
746280	Pte.	Clark, F.	Port Perry, Ont.
2537330	Pte.	Clark, A.	Port Perry, Ont.
2562375	Pte.	Coates, W. J.	East Orange, U.S.A.
745344	Pte.	Congdon, O. J.	Atherley, Ont.
690804	Pte.	Cooke, W. F.	Hamilton, Ont.
264536	Pte.	Cooper, J. W.	Hamilton, Ont.
775460	Pte.	Corless, H. S.	Bolton, Ont.
642058	Pte.	Cole, B. T.	Orillia, Ont.
928416	Pte.	Cole, W. F.	Surrey, England
249711	Pte.	Cowan, A. F. C.	Toronto, Ont.
775467	Pte.	Cousins, W. J.	Brampton, Ont.
3107044	Pte.	Colling, J. H.	Darlington, Eng.
3031118	Pte.	Courtney, G. B.	Paterson, N.J.
690038	Pte.	Crampton, F.	Hamilton, Ont.
690342	Pte.	Crisp, J. P.	Hamilton, Ont.
690268	Pte.	Crockett, H. G.	Abbotsford, B.C.
249251	Pte.	Crosthwait, W. H.	Dublin, Ireland
3106722	Pte.	Currie, J. D.	Gore Bay, Ont.
690873	Pte.	Dale, E. N.	Marlbank, Ont.
775054	Pte.	Davey, S. J.	Toronto, Ont.
678564	Pte.	Davis, G. F.	Toronto, Ont.
678078	Pte.	Dewes, L.	Toronto, Ont.
3106206	Pte.	Delauney, L. A.	Mexico City, Mex.
868273	Pte.	De Geer, C. W.	Uxbridge, Ont.

HONOR ROLL

Regt. No.	Rank	Name	Address
3106579	Pte.	Delien, A. A..............	Hóboken, N.J.
644576	Pte.	Desroches, H..............	Penetanguishene,Ont.
775914	Pte.	Dixon, T. W..............	Toronto, Ont.
3106727	Pte.	Dobbs, N..............	Dunchurch, Ont.
690395	Pte.	Downton, H. V..............	Hamilton, Ont.
678809	Pte.	Douglas, F. W..............	Pelham, Herts, Eng.
868170	Pte.	Doubt, A. B..............	Port Perry, Ont.
3105438	Pte.	Downey, J..............	Yorks, England.
2562420	Pte.	Douglass, F..............	Walton, England
3025022	Pte.	Dowling, P..............	Lisanearla, Ireland
644579	Pte.	Dusome, K. H..............	Penetanguishene,Ont.
228432	Pte.	Earnshaw, B. A..............	Toronto, Ont.
690764	Pte.	Eastwood, H.`K..............	Hamilton, Ont.
3105356	Pte.	Edwards, D. D..............	Freeport, Maine
681617	Pte.	Edwards, F. W..............	Toronto, Ont.
3105612	Pte.	Ede, A. E..............	Niagara Falls S., Ont.
3106823	Pte.	Elder, G. C..............	Hudson Bay Jct.,Sask.
644454	Pte.	Ellery, H. M..............	Wyebridge, Ont.
643877	Pte.	Elson, Charles..............	Ibstock, England
340136	Pte.	Emery, C..............	Toronto, Ont.
663460	Pte.	Ewing, R. E..............	Laurel, Ont.
690276	Pte.	Fairbrother, L..............	Hamilton, Ont.
745373	Pte.	Fairman, J. J..............	Argyle, Ont.
225373	Pte.	Fester, Arthur D..............	McNab, Ont.
238121	Pte.	Flaherty, Charles J..............	Guelph, Ont.
648321	Pte.	Flanigan, W. J..............	Heaslip, Ont.
2507364	Pte.	Fogarty, M..............	Ireland
237015	Pte.	Fortner, E..............	Toronto, Ont.
264532	Pte.	Forrest, T. W..............	Brooklyn, N.Y.

Regt. No.	Rank	Name	Address
868434	Pte.	Foster, C.	Oshawa, Ont.
2537469	Pte.	Fox, J. J.	Liverpool, Eng.
757526	Pte.	Forbes, G. H. E.	Hamilton, Ont.
225283	Pte.	Foster, W. C.	Pittsburgh, Pa.
757988	Pte.	Fraser, G. E.	Hamilton, Ont.
528082	Pte.	Frisken, G. W.	Toronto, Ont.
458095	Pte.	Fuller, J.	Montreal, Que.
192025	Pte.	Fulton, A.	London, Eng.
2537467	Pte.	Galer, G. F.	Wangford, England
644464	Pte.	Gardiner, V.	Midland, Ont.
690399	Pte.	Gatenby, A.	Hamilton, Ont.
226462	Pte.	Gates, J. A.	Detroit, Mich.
663093	Pte.	Gillard, F. G.	Mount Hamilton, Ont.
746468	Pte.	Gittings, F. J.	Manor, Sask.
249379	Pte.	Gibson, R. J.	Toronto, Ont.
679080	Pte.	Ginn, A. G.	Toronto, Ont.
3030541	Pte.	Givens, F. R.	Blairstown, N.J.
3105361	Pte.	Gleason, P.	Philadelphia, Pa.
678827	Pte.	Gouldsbrough, F.	Durham, Eng.
690554	Pte.	Gordon, R.	Hamilton, Ont.
763042	Pte.	Goodall, H. H.	Warren, Ont.
2537359	Pte.	Gordon, D.	Aberdeen, Scotland
3030514	Pte.	Goodwin, H.	Chelsea, Mass.
3107089	Pte.	Goodstein, J.	Cleveland, Ohio
643883	Pte.	Gowanlock, J. L.	Atherley, Ont.
678586	Pte.	Graham, C.	Toronto, Ont.
690661	Pte.	Graisley, T. V.	Hamilton, Ont.
745072	Pte.	Greenwood, F. H.	Sunderland, Ont.
868329	Pte.	Greenwood, D. N.	Sunderland, Ont.

HONOR ROLL 103

Regt. No.	Rank	Name	Address
3030303	Pte.	Greenwood, J. A............	Philadelphia, Pa.
3005310	Pte.	Greene, J......................	Toronto, Ont.
690513	Pte.	Guthrie, J......................	Hamilton, Ont.
681303	Pte.	Hadley, S. K.................	Ilkley, Yorks, Eng.
690403	Pte.	Harvey, C. E.................	Hamilton, Ont.
237903	Pte.	Halpin, W.....................	Glen William, Ont.
678329	Pte.	Halfyard, W. R.............	Toronto, Ont.
769948	Pte.	Hardy, A.......................	Bradford, Yorks, Eng.
690285	Pte.	Hartley, B.....................	Hamilton, Ont.
264234	Pte.	Haslam, H.....................	Retford, Notts, Eng.
775711	Pte.	Hadden, W. J................	Toronto, Ont.
3105135	Pte.	Hawkes, R....................	New Grafton, N.S.
868198	Pte.	Hall, R. H.....................	Sunderland, Ont.
264333	Pte.	Hamilton, W. J..............	Chicago, Ill.
3030159	Pte.	Haines, W. A.................	Freeport, Pa.
228195	Pte.	Hadden, G. A................	Newport, Eng.
868377	Pte.	Hazard, A. J..................	Oshawa, Ont.
1063009	Pte.	Heath, G. E...................	Manchester, Eng.
681264	Pte.	Heath, T.......................	Toronto, Ont.
663544	Pte.	Hewson, E. T................	Orangeville, Ont.
690078	Pte.	Henderson, E. F............	Hamilton, Ont.
3030392	Pte.	Hennigan, W. T............	Philadelphia, Pa.
644065	Pte.	Herbert, S. A.................	Hawkestone, Ont.
758034	Pte.	Hill, W. E.....................	Hamilton, Ont.
644586	Pte.	Hirst, C. H....................	Penetanguishene, Ont.
3030441	Pte.	Hicks, J.........................	Toronto, Ont.
679102	Pte.	Hogarth, J.....................	Toronto, Ont.
250058	Pte.	Hopcraft, E. W..............	Toronto, Ont.
766850	Pte.	House, W. J..................	Toronto, Ont.

Regt. No.	Rank	Name	Address
3105443	Pte.	Hogan, J.	Chicago, Ill.
776085	Pte.	Howson, R. C.	Wingham, Ont.
514583	Pte.	Hunter, W. E.	Hamilton, Ont.
690934	Pte.	Hunter, R.	Tillicoultry, Scot.
746290	Pte.	Hull, W. H.	Oshawa, Ont.
663431	Pte.	Hutchins, F. C.	Illbury, Herts, Eng.
663022	Pte.	Hunt, E.	Burlington, Ont.
690077	Pte.	Hyland, F.	Cobourg, Ont.
663462	Pte.	Irwin, J. D.	Laurel, Ont.
678754	Pte.	Jackson, O. G.	Toronto, Ont.
3105288	Pte.	Jamieson, A.	Belfast, Ireland
679111	Pte.	Jeffery, A. G.	Lowerbourne, Eng.
3030654	Pte.	Jeulin, A. C.	New York, N.Y.
264247	Pte.	Johnson, W. M. (M.M.)	Calumet, Mich.
135747	Pte.	Johnson, A. R.	Stapenhill, England
644482	Pte.	Jones, G. A.	Vasey, Ont.
1063054	Pte.	Jones, I. W.	Apsley, Ont.
643899	Pte.	Jones, G. H.	Orillia, Ont.
757569	Pte.	Jones, R. A.	Hamilton, Ont.
3030579	Pte.	Jones, W.	Llandudno, Wales
727436	Pte.	Jones, A.	Stratford, Ont.
2507318	Pte.	Jones, J. H.	Flint, N. Wales
3105191	Pte.	Juleff, Wm. M.	England
928143	Pte.	Keith, J. A.	Simcoe, Ont.
3106189	Pte.	Kelly, J. E.	Springfield, Ill.
644850	Pte.	Kemp, H. J.	Wyebridge, Ont.
644591	Pte.	Kennedy, W.	Penetang, Ont.
644479	Pte.	Kinch, I. T. R.	Midland, Ont.
249509	Pte.	King, P.	Rossport, Ont.

HONOR ROLL 105

Regt. No.	Rank	Name	Address
2537472	Pte.	King, R. P.	Philadelphia, Pa.
264098	Pte.	Kubiak, M.	Detroit, Mich.
644070	Pte.	Lamble, W. R.	Orillia, Ont.
644018	Pte.	Langley, J. M.	Lawson, Ont.
2507404	Pte.	Lannigan, W. H.	Chicago, Ill.
1090239	Pte.	Laronde, T. A.	Cobalt, Ont.
850091	Pte.	Lawn, P.	Braintree, Essex, Eng.
680204	Pte.	Lee, A.	Toronto, Ont.
775944	Pte.	Leece, W. T.	Brampton, Ont.
642700	Pte.	Legg, A. W.	New Lowell
228049	Pte.	Lillew, H. W.	Toronto, Ont.
775736	Pte.	Litchfield, T. W.	Toronto, Ont.
678033	Pte.	Litherland, A. O. H.	Toronto, Ont.
678619	Pte.	Lloyd, W. E.	Toronto, Ont.
678621	Pte.	Logan, W.	Toronto, Ont.
264187	Pte.	Loughlin, T.	Los Angeles, Cal.
3105101	Pte.	Lowe, A.	Evanston, Ill.
663182	Pte.	Lowman, R.	London, England
3317073	Pte.	Luney, T. W.	Toronto, Ont.
249456	Pte.	Mangan, M. E.	Dublin, Ireland
249731	Pte.	Machin, J. E.	Toronto, Ont.
644072	Pte.	Marshall, F.	Orillia, Ont.
690307	Pte.	Massey, P. A.	Hamilton, Ont.
690838	Pte.	Macklow, J. A.	Hamilton, Ont.
757849	Pte.	May, J. W.	Hamilton, Ont.
663780	Pte.	Maples, R. F.	Mono Mills, Ont.
868237	Pte.	Marshall, R. J.	Wilberforce, Ont.
3106003	Pte.	MacIntosh, A. G.	Jersey City, N.J.
2529441	Pte.	Mayne, C. J.	Toronto, Ont.

THE 116TH BATTALION IN FRANCE

Regt. No.	Rank	Name	Address
249452	Pte.	McPhail, J......................	Toronto, Ont.
249140	Pte.	McGrath, H. P.............	Toronto, Ont.
237630	Pte.	McDade, J......................	Toronto, Ont.
690573	Pte.	McFarlane, W...............	Hamilton, Ont.
3030274	Pte.	McCallum, W...............	Philadelphia, Pa.
757870	Pte.	McInnes, D. G...............	Hamilton, Ont.
644074	Pte.	McNabb, C. H................	Orillia, Ont.
745428	Pte.	McMillan, J. A................	Beaverton, Ont.
690758	Pte.	McCall, W......................	Hamilton, Ont.
868051	Pte.	McInally, C.....................	Oshawa, Ont.
663553	Pte.	McLellan, E. W.............	Shelburne, Ont.
663187	Pte.	McGillivray, F. S...........	Orangeville, Ont.
745431	Pte.	McPhadden, C. R.........	Sunderland, Ont.
775989	Pte.	McCaffrey, W. L............	Caledon East, Ont.
3106214	Pte.	McArthur, T. A..............	Kansas City, Mo.
264540	Pte.	McKay, J. G. (M.M.)...	Cincinnati, Ohio
3105335	Pte.	McCord, R......................	Danville, Que.
3030969	Pte.	McGrath, J. P................	Chicago, Ill.
3030533	Pte.	McLean, D......................	Philadelphia, Pa.
3105497	Pte.	McTavish, R. A.............	Glasgow, Scotland
2304372	Pte.	McKissock, D................	Johnstone, Scotland
3107124	Pte.	McCrea, F......................	Chicago, Ill.
3106002	Pte.	McCaig, H.....................	Toronto, Ont.
3106304	Pte.	McKee, A.......................	Ballymoney, Ireland
663186	Pte.	McDonald, J. W............	Grand Valley, Ont.
3310318	Pte.	Merkley, W. S................	Dundas, Ont.
2537304	Pte.	Methuen, W...................	Dunfermline, Scot.
678877	Pte.	Middleton, W. J............	Toronto, Ont.
172359	Pte.	Miller, F. O....................	Toronto, Ont.

HONOR ROLL

Regt. No.	Rank	Name	Address
249286	Pte.	Miller, F. L.	Toronto, Ont.
644829	Pte.	Montgomery, J. C.	Midland, Ont.
690229	Pte.	Montgomery, W. J. A.	Hamilton, Ont.
679133	Pte.	Montgomery, E. J.	Toronto, Ont.
3106407	Pte.	Morrison, J. J.	Hamilton, Ont.
857010	Pte.	Moore, W.	London, Eng.
746465	Pte.	Moore, G. E.	Burketon, Ont.
681188	Pte.	Morgan, C. W.	Walsall, Staffs., Eng.
663751	Pte.	Mottart, H. A.	Waldemar, Ont.
3030309	Pte.	Morgan, J.	Bellevue, Pa.
448714	Pte.	Moore, A.	Montreal, Que.
3030279	Pte.	Mulligan, J. J.	Ballagfraderrin, Ire.
690734	Pte.	Muldoon, P.	Linwood, Scot.
2537499	Pte.	Murphy, A. L.	St. John's, Nfld.
3105661	Pte.	Noonan, T.	Chicago, Ill.
3105019	Pte.	O'Donnelly, D. S.	Hamilton, Ont.
529289	Pte.	O'Leary, J. P.	Detroit, Mich.
1003244	Pte.	Oliver, W. F.	Thessalon, Ont.
273632	Pte.	O'Neill, J.	Liverpool, Eng.
2537416	Pte.	Orr, W.	Stockport, England
679152	Pte.	Osborne, S.	Bristol, England
746072	Pte.	Owen, J.	Beeton, Ont.
678203	Pte.	Park, L. C.	Toronto, Ont.
690798	Pte.	Park, R.	Glasgow, Scotland
757924	Pte.	Parish, H. J.	Hamilton, Ont.
678651	Pte.	Parker, F.	Toronto, Ont.
679283	Pte.	Patterson, M.	Kilmacnenan, Ireland
678088	Pte.	Painter, W. J.	Toronto, Ont.
644519	Pte.	Paul, H.	Midland, Ont.

Regt. No.	Rank	Name	Address
678894	Pte.	Payne, A. E. S.	Bradford, Yorks,Eng.
3105507	Pte.	Paylor, G. F.	Lynn, Mass.
733605	Pte.	Pearl, A. M.	Berwick, N. S.
775906	Pte.	Perkins, C.	Clawton, England
3106172	Pte.	Perks, E.	St. John's, Nfld.
644094	Pte.	Phillips, V. R.	Orillia, Ont.
678898	Pte.	Philip, R. M.	Toronto, Ont.
2537366	Pte.	Pink, S.	Farnham, England
171997	Pte.	Pimlott, H.	Toronto, Ont.
3106293	Pte.	Plooard, T. A.	Hamilton, Ont.
663668	Pte.	Potter, N. C.	Waldemar, Ont.
3105758	Pte.	Powell, F.	Chicago, Ill.
868420	Pte.	Pritchard, L. H.	Ramsgate, England
644518	Pte.	Puddicomb, W. J.	Midland, Ont.
690246	Pte.	Pulsford, F. J.	Hamilton, Ont.
643948	Pte.	Raaflaub, R. O.	Jarrett, Ont.
3105793	Pte.	Ramsey, J.	Hillhead Faroes,Scot.
663514	Pte.	Rainey, F. W.	Grand Valley, Ont.
3314394	Pte.	Randle, W.	Bridgeburg, Ont.
745612	Pte.	Reesor, I. O.	Cedar Grove, Ont.
679161	Pte.	Reid, A. E.	Toronto, Ont.
679164	Pte.	Reid, L.	Toronto, Ont.
3310211	Pte.	Ribble, G. A.	Walsingham C., Ont.
690645	Pte.	Rogers, W. C.	St. Ann's, Ont.
240616	Pte.	Robertson, D. E.	Hamilton, Ont.
690621	Pte.	Rorie, T.	Hamilton, Ont.
690158	Pte.	Rogers, J. T.	Hamilton, Ont.
746118	Pte.	Sayers, J.	Cedardale, Ont.
457964	Pte.	Sauve, W.	Montreal, Que.

HONOR ROLL

Regt. No.	Rank	Name	Address
3031164	Pte.	Sather, O..............	Denver, Col.
3030180	Pte.	Sandell, W..............	Philadelphia, Pa.
3030837	Pte.	Sanderson, R. F..............	Oconomowoc, Wis.
1004236	Pte.	Sandie, E. C..............	Thessalon, Ont.
642072	Pte.	Scott, P. H..............	Orillia, Ont.
3106266	Pte.	Shuman, O. G..............	Eldorado, Ill.
2393428	Pte.	Secker, A. E..............	London, Eng.
3314848	Pte.	Shannon, F. R..............	Collingwood, Ont.
745472	Pte.	Sheffield, J. H..............	Udora, Ont.
643407	Pte.	Sharp, J. J..............	Tottenham, Ont.
868119	Pte.	Shaw, A. H..............	Toronto, Ont.
763406	Pte.	Shortt, E. S..............	Muskoka, Ont.
249661	Pte.	Shier, H. E..............	Pefferlaw, Ont.
3106366	Pte.	Sholters, G. H..............	Cainsville, Ont.
663515	Pte.	Simmons, A. R..............	Dundalk, Ont.
754471	Pte.	Smith, H. A..............	Toronto, Ont.
644710	Pte.	Sproule, H. T..............	Penetang, Ont.
644867	Pte.	Sterrett, A. W..............	London, Eng.
775564	Pte.	Stronge, A..............	Toronto, Ont.
249634	Pte.	Stephenson, J. B..............	Toronto, Ont.
681865	Pte.	Stott, T..............	Toronto, Ont.
868113	Pte.	Stone, A. W..............	Greenbank, Ont.
797616	Pte.	Stipe, C. L..............	Delhi, Ont.
250141	Pte.	Stout, J. P..............	Toronto, Ont.
679188	Pte.	Switzer, R. G..............	Toronto, Ont.
802471	Pte.	Swan, J..............	London, Ont.
644533	Pte.	Symons, F. A..............	Midland, Ont.
868019	Pte.	Taylor, A. L..............	St. Catharines, Ont.
3317099	Pte.	Tennison, J. W..............	Sebright, Ont.

Regt. No.	Rank	Name	Address
3105825	Pte.	Thomson, A.	Jeanette, Pa.
3105824	Pte.	Toon, G. W.	Chicago, Ill.
690974	Pte.	Toner, E.	Carlisle, England
868053	Pte.	Trick, I. J.	Oshawa, Ont.
690643	Pte.	Turnbull, T.	Hamilton, Ont.
757649	Pte.	Unsworth, R.	Hamilton, Ont.
644628	Pte.	Vailliancourt, J.	Penetanguishene, Ont.
2562460	Pte.	Vallis, A. H.	N. Devon., Bermuda
757472	Pte.	Vanevery, M.	Niagara Falls, Ont.
644630	Pte.	Vasseur, A. P.	Penetanguishene, Ont.
746446	Pte.	Wain, L. A.	Uxbridge, Ont.
457552	Pte.	Walsh, S.	Montreal, Que.
690625	Pte.	Waters, H. J.	Hamilton, Ont.
775592	Pte.	Walker, A.	Palgrave, Ont.
803030	Pte.	Walters, J. W.	Thorndale, Ont.
157527	Pte.	Waller, J.	Toronto, Ont.
225715	Pte.	Wallis, I. N.	Greensville, Ont.
1090125	Pte.	Weaver, E.	Picton, Ont.
690599	Pte.	Wells, A. E.	Yarmouth, Eng.
1090410	Pte.	Webb, G.	Arlington, N.J.
757935	Pte.	Weir, A. G.	Burford, Ont.
775589	Pte.	West, J. T.	Brampton, Ont.
690841	Pte.	Welsh, Bert.	Hamilton, Ont.
3034652	Pte.	Westerman, E. W.	Buffalo, N.Y.
681513	Pte.	White, J. B.	Toronto, Ont.
757658	Pte.	White, J.	London, England
745500	Pte.	Whetter, F.	Woodville, Ont.
2529450	Pte.	Wilson, R. McK.	Paris, Ont.
1090151	Pte.	Wilkins, E.	Picton, Ont.

HONOR ROLL

Regt. No.	Rank	Name	Address
850618	Pte.	Williamson, J. C.	Thorold, Ont.
690204	Pte.	Wilson, A. S.	Hamilton, Ont.
264615	Pte.	Wilson, H. T.	Parkersburg, W. Va.
643981	Pte.	Williams, W. J.	Longford, Ont.
237243	Pte.	Williams, G. E.	Toronto, Ont.
285570	Pte.	Wood, T.	Scotland
775584	Pte.	Wood, W. H.	Bolton, Ont.
3106755	Pte.	Woodcock, J. O.	Dwight, Ont.
1090068	Pte.	Wylie, B.	Brinston, Ont.
225462	Pte.	Yaffo, N. W.	Toronto, Ont.

www.ingramcontent.com/pod-product-compliance
Lightning Source LLC
Chambersburg PA
CBHW060837190426
43197CB00040B/2662